the complete **kitchen** garden

the complete **kitchen** garden

the art of designing and planting an edible garden

Patrick Bowe

photographs by Cynthia Woodyard

Macmillan • USA

MACMILLAN
A Simon & Schuster Macmillan Company
1633 Broadway
New York, NY 10019

Library of Congress Cataloging-in-Publication Data

Bowe, Patrick.
        The complete kitchen garden : the art of designing and planting an edible
    garden / Patrick Bowe ; photographs by Cynthia Woodyard.
            p.   cm.
        Includes bibliographical references (p.   ) and index.
        ISBN 0-02-861309-0
        1. Edible landscaping.   2. Gardens—Design.   I. Title.
        SB475.9.E35B68   1996
        712' .6—dc20   96-21787
                                                                      CIP

Manufactured in the United States of America
10 9 8 7 6 5 4 3 2 1

Design by Amy Peppler Adams—designLab, Seattle

Acknowledgments

With thanks to all of the garden owners and to: John Barstow, Nicola Gordon Bowe, Frances-Jane French, Derek Hill, Penelope Hobhouse, Joy Larkcom, John Meils, Mrs. Paul Mellon, Helen Pratt, The Marchioness of Salisbury, George Stacpoole, Comtesse Nanda d'Ursel, Rosemary Verey, and Jacques Wirtz.

Contents

Foreword by Rosemary Verey ix

Introduction 1

Planning and Design 13

Site Selection and Size   15
Beds, Paths, and Edges   23
Walls, Fences, and Hedges   51
Arbors, Arches, and Tunnels   69
Greenhouses, Potting Sheds,
and Garden Houses   89
Seats and Other Garden Ornaments   99

Planting 119

Designing with Fruits and Vegetables 121
Color, Form, and Texture in the
Kitchen Garden   147
Conclusion   181

Resources 187

Suppliers of Seeds and Plants   188
Kitchen Gardens Open to the Public   192
Suggested Reading   195

Index 199

Gardens Featured in the Text

U.S.A. and Canada

Les Quatre Vents, Quebec (Mr. and Mrs. Frank Cabot)

Falls Village, Connecticut (Mrs. Nancy McCabe)

Lakeville, Connecticut (Mrs. Elise Lufkin)

Walnut Creek, California (Mudd's Restaurant)

England

Hillbarn House, Wiltshire
(Mr. and Mrs. Alastair Buchanan)

Stavordale Priory, Somerset (Mr. and Mrs. Langton)

Sudborough Old Rectory, Northhamptonshire
(Mr. and Mrs. Huntington)

Highgrove, Gloucestershire (H.R.H., The Prince of Wales)

Barnsley House, Gloucestershire (Mrs. Rosemary Verey)

France

La Coquetterie, Normandy
(M. and Mme. Adalbert de Bagneux)

Le Manoir de Criqueboeuf, Normandy (Mrs. Yul Brynner)

Villandry, Loire Valley (The Carvalho Family)

La Petite Fontanille, Provence
(Ambassador Ann Cox Chambers)

The Netherlands

Te Doom, Veerlen
(Mrs. Ineke Greve)

Foreword

BY ROSEMARY VEREY

Today, it is easy to slip into the supermarket to buy a bag of brussels sprouts or a cabbage. As we pile them into our shopping carts, do we consider when they were picked or read the label *Use by...*? Often I wonder how many of my fellow shoppers have seen brussels sprouts growing on their sturdy stems.

There was a time when every country person grew enough vegetables to feed a family and a horse-drawn cart laden with freshly picked vegetables went regularly through the streets for townspeople to patronize. In those days, people could be sure that no noxious sprays or artificial fertilizers had been used on them. We cannot turn back the clock, but many people today are realizing the importance and pleasure of growing and eating their own fresh vegetables.

Books about kitchen gardens give advice on sowing seeds and how many inches apart the brassicas should be planted. However, most fail to tell about the excitement of watching seeds germinate and pea pods swell, or the fun of creating color schemes with red and green lettuces, scarlet runner beans, and amazing gourds.

This book is different. Both Patrick Bowe, the author, and Cynthia Woodyard, the photographer, are practical gardeners, but they have also absorbed ideas from horticulturists, historians, and artists of earlier centuries. Even more important, they have brought their own great artistry to these pages.

Common sense based on practical experience pervades the book. Advice about selecting your site and improving your soil is sound and helpful, and the author points out that protection from the prevailing wind is as important as considering ways to combat frost. The landscaping and architectural elements—treatment of beds, paths, walls, and arbors, discussion of greenhouses, suggestions for garden ornaments—give facts and advice that readers will really want to know in clear, simple, and economic terms. It is a model of helpful garden writing. Where an artist's eye and creativity are called for—when you start to design patterns for your beds and paths or select fruit and vegetables to associate in harmony or contrast—Patrick Bowe inspires you to make your own choices.

I particularly like the way all this good advice is interspersed with descriptions of actual kitchen gardens—in the United States, Canada, and Europe. Ideas become reality as you study Cynthia Woodyard's splendid photographs of La Petite Fontanille in France, Hillbarn House in England, or Les Quatres Vents in Canada. Some of these gardens are unknown, but they all capture the vision of form, color enjoyment, and mouthwatering arrays of vegetable displays that belong at the heart of any good book about vegetable gardening.

I only wish that Patrick and Cynthia's book had been available twenty years ago when I embarked on our Barnsley potager; it would have saved me many hours of pondering. It will bring home to you the beauty of flowers combined with vegetables and inspire you to read the old authors who wrote for the country housewives. Then, vegetable gardening was a necessity—today it is a pleasure.

Rosemary Verey
March 1996

Introduction

This is an exciting time in garden history because a new form of ornamental gardening has become available to us. For centuries, the kitchen garden was the "Cinderella" of gardening, of interest only on a practical level. Now, as a result of many technical developments and a fascinating leap of the human imagination, it has arrived at the forefront of contemporary garden design.

The kitchen garden has been evolving slowly, in many parts of the world, under the hands and eyes of many distinguished gardeners.This book brings together for the first time the many strands of this development and presents a coherent picture of this new garden form. The book's aim is to focus exclusively on the movement's aesthetic aspects and to ignore, except in so far as they strongly determine design, the practical methods of cultivation. These methods

Left: The complex patterns of paths and vegetable beds at Villandry are best appreciated when seen from above.

have been the subject of many books in the past and information on them is now widely available.

It was the tragic accident of war in 1914 that compelled Joachim and Ann Carvalho to substitute vegetables for the formal bedding plants planned for their new parterre at Villandry in France. It was their imaginative arrangement and the hitherto unexperienced patterns of form, color, and texture that resulted in the first steps toward the development of the new ornamental kitchen garden. Villandry transformed our view of kitchen gardens, but it was a vast conception far beyond the capacity of the average gardener. What has happened since—the development of increasingly dwarf forms of fruit and vegetables, such as

Right: Semicircular arbors covered with climbing roses mark the path intersection.

Below: Powerful visual rhythms are established with lines of 'Drumhead' cabbages.

step-over and maypole fruit trees, and fast-growing and "pixie" salad crops—has brought Villandry's principles, not to speak of its bounty and variety, within reach of even the backyard gardener.

The current popularity of the kitchen garden has been further propelled by (1) the development of new disease-free, pest-resistant, more quickly maturing, and longer-lasting strains of vegetables and fruit and (2) the revival of the raised-bed system of cultivation, which has transformed kitchen gardening from a back-breaking, mini-

agricultural enterprise into an activity whose reduced physical demands have brought it within reach of everyone.

As a result of easy travel and communication, a "global village" has been created, making a whole range of vegetable and fruit seed available. For example, newly introduced oriental vegetables can now be seen in American and European gardens growing alongside dwarf sweet corn from Seattle and new salad varieties from Italy. Such expanded availability of seed material has enabled pioneering gardeners to experiment with new edible plant combinations for both aesthetic and practical effects. The palette of color, texture, and form available to the kitchen garden designer is ever increasing as new plants and varieties are introduced.

Combining beauty with utility, the ornamental kitchen garden responds to the New Puritanism of our time. The arbitrariness of many modern gardening styles can be replaced by a sound foundation of practical necessity. In the contemporary kitchen gar-

den, form closely follows function—solidly built paths, narrow beds, and sheltering fences are determined by strict, utilitarian demands. It is also a form of garden that responds to the new emphasis on a more integrated lifestyle, combining the many enjoyable physical activities of gardening, cooking, and eating, with exercise of the intellect and imagination.

Above: Cool vegetable tones are heightened with bright flower color.

Right: The elegant baroque detailing of the latticework arbors.

Barnsley House,
Gloucestershire, England

ROSEMARY VEREY

The new kitchen garden was born at Barnsley, the Cotswold manor house of one of today's most original gardeners, Rosemary Verey. The idea began to evolve over eighteen years ago, when she was becoming bored with her old-fashioned, conventional vegetable garden. As she pored over her rich collection of antique gardening books, she found her inspiration in William Lawson's seventeenth-century work, *The Country Housewife's Garden*. He recommended growing vegetables in small beds no more than five feet wide, so that "the weeder women can go between." There was an illustration of the kind of plan he had in mind.

The kitchen garden is divided into a network of easily accessible beds.

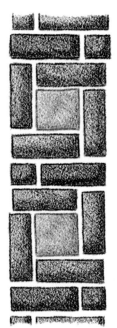

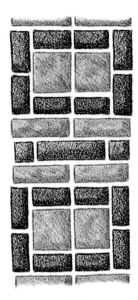

13½"

18"

18"

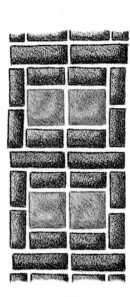

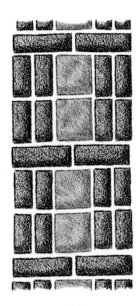

.18"

18"

18"

6" x 6" stone tile

9" x 3" red brick

9" x 3" black brick

Brick and tile paving patterns for paths at
Barnsley House.

Above: Rosemary Verey gives a sense of height to her design by introducing a vegetable tunnel on which grow climbing vegetables like gourds and lablab beans.

Below: Brick paths wear well under the tough conditions of a kitchen garden. Box cones at the bed corners add visual definition.

Rosemary Verey took pen to squared paper and drew a plan loosely based on Lawson's. It was for a garden seventy-five feet square, no bigger than is necessary to feed one family, and capable of being tended by

one person. She then marked out her plan on site before making the final adjustments, as the American landscape architect, Beatrix Farrand advised.

The overall plan is divided into four quarters like the Paradise gardens of old. The four-quarter division is, by coincidence, ideally suited to the vegetable garden with its four-fold crop rotation. Realizing that the paths between the many small beds would take a lot of wear, she decided to construct them in brick—old brick with character, culled from demolition sites, *not* super-smooth, newly manufactured brick. She wrote:

> *To have bought all new materials would have been more than my budget would stand, so we did it gradually, finding old bricks when buildings were pulled down. The local blacksmith's forge was closed and we were allowed the lovely black industrial bricks from that floor. Most buildings around us were built in stone, but eventually we found a red brick house being demolished and took as many of these as we could.*

Right: Apples on dwarfing rootstock are trained into a "closed goblet" form, another height-giving element in the design.

Below: Standard gooseberries generate a powerful visual rhythm along the central garden path.

Back in her garden, she decided to lay her brick paths on a sand base, not on the more conventional and stable concrete base. In time, the bricks have settled, giving the look she wanted—deliberately casual and non-professional. She used bricks of three different colors and created a different pattern for each path. This gives a strong visual impact and successfully holds the design together, especially during the winter months when the beds are virtually empty. Each brick color was chosen carefully—the stone colors reflect the honey-colored Cotswold walls, the black matches the heavily manured and composted soil, and the red adds warmth.

Rosemary Verey quickly recognized a design problem: vegetables lack height. To achieve this essential element, she used climbing vegetables and fruit trees. At one end of the Barnsley garden, lablab beans and gourds have been set to grow over a series of hoops, making a vegetable tunnel. Underneath are planted coneflowers, nasturtiums, and sunflowers. The runner beans share the hoops with the gourds and then climb up the tall stems of the sunflowers. In other spots, golden hop and purple vine grow over wooden arbors designed to shelter seats—indispensable on a hot day in the kitchen garden. Fruit trees give height in a variety of ways. Apples are trained to 8-foot-high metal

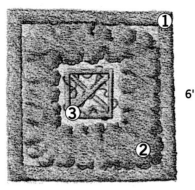

6'

6'

1. Dwarf box edging
2. Beetroot 'Bolthardy'
3. Scarlet runner beans on bamboo obelisk

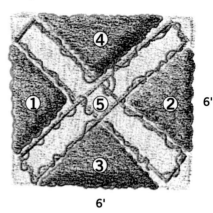

6'

6'

1. Lettuce radicchio 'Cesare'
2. Lettuce 'Mizura'
3./4. Parsley
5. St. Andrew's Cross in bamboo canes with scarlet runner beans

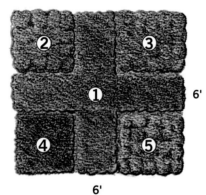

6'

6'

1. Sweet corn
2. Lettuce 'Napa Valley'
3. Lettuce 'Noquette'
4. Giant red mustard
5. Lettuce 'Baby Purchia'

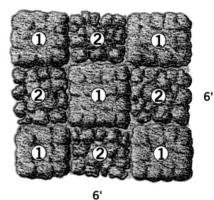

6'

6'

1. Lettuce 'Red Grenobloise'
2. Blue-green leeks 'Musselborough'

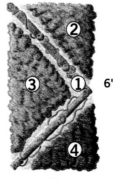

6'

3'

1. Apple cordons
2. Corn salad 'Vert de Cambrai'
3. Sprouts 'Bedford Fillbasket'
4. Broccoli 'Dwarf Curled'

"goblets," an idea culled from Louis XIV's kitchen garden at Versailles. Dwarf 'Victoria' plums are trained up, then out and down to form what are known as festoons. Dwarf pears are grown as low, step-over "cordons" to give shelter to newly emerging seedlings. Soft fruit is also used to give height. For example, standard gooseberries, planted among the lavender hedges that line the central path, are clipped into balls of foliage growing above a bare stem. Standard 'Iceberg' roses, hollies, and hawthorns are also used for height where the design requires. (The hawthorns and hollies echo the hedgerow plants in the surrounding fields.)

For the actual planting of the garden, Rosemary Verey turned to the great French kitchen garden of Villandry for inspiration. There, since 1914, the Carvalho family has been demonstrating to an incredulous gardening world that vegetables, if thoughtfully arranged in an ornamental fashion, can be as attractive as flowers. She wrote:

> *Once you start thinking of planting your vegetables in a decorative way, in color and texture patterns, you will enjoy working in the garden. One of the great joys of having small beds is the fun of thinking up new plant combinations each year.*

In planning these vegetable combinations, she takes full advantage of the ease of worldwide communications today. Dwarf sweet corn grown from seed obtained in Seattle may be interplanted with Chinese bok choy or Italian lettuce and mulched with crushed cocoa shells from Africa. Many such new plant combinations are possible in today's vegetable garden, but some that Rosemary Verey has found especially successful are:

Red and golden beetroot	Plant in alternate rows or blocks to give a stunning checkerboard pattern.
Swiss and ruby chard	The combination is worthy of the flower garden. The stems of ruby chard with the sun shining through them have a color as brilliant as anything in the flower garden.
Purple sprouts with lettuce	Purple brussels sprouts interplanted with green give vivid contrast.
'Christmas' and 'Drumhead' cabbages	Interplanted, they give a purple and green stippled effect. As both mature late in the year, they can be cropped together and the ground left ready for spring sowing.
Leeks 'Musselborough' and cabbage 'Scarlett O'Hara'	Interplant to give a textural and formal contrast but a glaucous-blue color harmony.
Cabbage 'Greyhound' and dwarf lavender	A cabbage bed edged with dwarf lavender gives textural contrast but silver-gray harmony.
Lettuce with strawberries	Interplant so that the strawberry runners will spread in late summer to cover the bare soil left by the lettuce cropping.
Mixed chicory	Thin out unwanted colors as they grow; the 'Verona' variety is especially useful when treated this way.

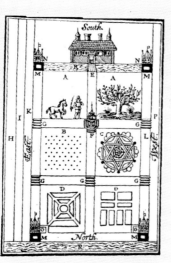

Right: A plan of a typical manor house garden from William Lawson's *New Orchard and Garden* (1618). The "A" squares show topiary figures and an espalier, "B" represents fruit trees, "C" is the knot garden, and the "D" squares show shaped kitchen garden beds.

A tip that will ensure a garden's attractiveness is to surround the beds with an edging, which will act as a visual frame to the interior plantings. It will also help keep the garden neat by preventing soil spillage on paths during digging or manuring, and it will give a small amount of shelter to young seedlings after they have been transplanted. Parsley, chives, alpine strawberries, and box in many forms, common, dwarf, and variegated, are used as bed edgings at Barnsley. When box is used, it is clipped into cones at the corners of the beds to give strong visual definition. Dwarf forms of lettuce are also used on a temporary, annual basis.

The appearance of the vegetable bed in winter should be kept in mind when creating a planting scheme, Rosemary Verey cautions. Winter vegetables like leeks, onions, winter cabbage, and brussels sprouts can be set out to make their own decorative patterns when all the other vegetables have been

Below: A pair of clipped variegated privets punctuate a bed of sweet corn and Swiss chard, and a self-sown hollyhock creates a visual break among the well-ordered rows of vegetables. A hop-covered arbor provides the background.

Plan of Barnsley house kitchen garden based on the plan from Lawson's *New Orchard and Garden*.

cropped or have died down. Empty beds can be dressed immediately after cropping, adding bark or leaf mulch, manure or compost as required for the next year's crop. As a result, each bed will look not only tidy, but different from its neighbors, contributing in a positive way to the design in spite of the season.

Although good husbandry demands that fruit and vegetables be set out in ordered rows, a regimented effect can be avoided by deliberately encouraging the occasional self-sown seedling. At Barnsley, viola, hollyhock, lupin, and allium seedlings volunteer from the neighboring flower garden, and some are allowed to remain. An occasional plant of last year's chicory is left to flower amid this year's lettuces. Stone crops and mosses flourish in the joints of the wall or paving. Potatoes too small for the table are left along the paths for mice and birds to eat. Colored bottles full of sugared water are set out to divert the wasps when the apples are ripening. Such incidental touches contribute to the garden's charm. The relaxed informality of this garden, which is located on a farm, is further enhanced by its not being enclosed within a set of uniformly designed walls. There are low Cotswold stone walls on two sides, but on the third is a cowbarn and on the fourth is a post-and-rail fence over which horses can be seen grazing in the adjoining field.

The garden at Barnsley was the first of the new kitchen gardens to be made, but it does not remain static. Each year, Rosemary Verey produces new and exciting vegetable combinations for the design, which makes visiting the garden a continuing inspiration.

Planning and Design

Site Selection and Size

The ideal site for a kitchen garden is a plot that is open but not exposed, sheltered by walls to the north and east. It should have a slight slope to the south but not a wall at the bottom of the slope, as this would trap cold air and create an unwelcome frost pocket. Few are blessed with such a perfect site.

Most will have to plan their kitchen gardens while accepting the inevitable compromises and adjustments associated with less-than-ideal conditions. The right mix of careful planning, consistent attention, and the proper choice of plants can result in a bountiful kitchen garden, one that pleases both the eye and the palate.

The following chapter will help you select the best location within the space available in your garden.

The ideal site for a new kitchen garden is an open but not exposed plot, exemplified by William Frederick's garden in Delaware.

A kitchen garden needs:

1. Sun:

    a. To ripen crops and encourage new growth on all fruit trees and other plants. Sunlight will also promote the development of fruit buds for next year's crop. (You can maximize this if your garden is on a slope by planting your fruit trees, not your vegetables, on high ground so they benefit from the maximum radiant and reflected sunlight.) Most fruits will tolerate up to a half-day's shade, but with reduced yields. Bush and cane fruits—raspberries and blackberries, in particular—have the highest tolerance for shade, provided the soil in which they are growing is not dry and there is no drip from overhanging trees. Lack of sunlight, although it restricts choice, is no excuse for avoiding fruit altogether.

    b. To grow tender, warm-weather crops like sweet corn and tomatoes, to over-winter vegetables in the ground, and to start early spring crops into growth while the angle of the sun is still low. (If you do have a vegetable garden with up to half a day of shade, all is not lost: using plastic cloches and frames will compensate for lack of sun by giving the early vegetables a warm start.)

    c. To give warmth for a small, south-facing greenhouse or frame. (If a corner of your kitchen garden *is* in total shade, put it to good use by locating your compost heap there. Then all the organic matter not used in your kitchen can be returned to the garden.)

Left: Mrs. Bunny Williams's garden in Connecticut is in shade for part of the day, but a careful choice of fruit varieties and the use of cloches to give seedlings a warm start compensates for a lack of sun.

Below: Mrs. Lufkin's kitchen garden in Lakeville, Connecticut, is ideally located in close proximity to the kitchen.

2. Good soil:

The ideal is a medium loam (a fertile mixture of clay and sand), usually dark in color and rich with humus. However, if your soil is not ideal, it can be improved. Light soils can be fed with generous applications of organic manure, which will increase the amount of water that soaks into the soil. Heavy, waterlogged soils can be lightened with similar applications of manure; a ditch dug around the site will help considerably to drain off excess water. Poorly drained soil severely restricts the range of vegetables you can grow, although it does not exclude the possibility of success with celery, fennel, and Chinese cabbage, which have their wild origins in marshland.

Apart from considering the quality of the soil when selecting a position for your kitchen garden, bear in mind that a level site makes working, and, in particular, pushing a wheelbarrow, easier. Finally, avoid a site with overhanging trees and shrubs, whose spreading roots will compete with those of your intended crops for nutrients and water.

3. Water:

A great proportion of all the fruit and vegetables we eat is water, normally supplied to the growing plants in the form of rain. In times of drought, it must be supplemented by artificial means. Investment in an underground supply of water to the kitchen garden will fully pay for itself during such times. Well-located taps or faucets will reduce the distances that water has to be carried or hoses trailed. However, tap water is often too cold to apply to tender young seedlings. For this reason, kitchen gardens in the past often incorporated pools or cisterns of standing water that were warmed by exposure to the ambient air temperature or the heat of the sun. The need for such a cistern can be turned to aesthetic advantage by the creation of an ornamental pool, which can provide a focal point at the center of the kitchen garden's design.

Sheltering trees on three sides of Mr. and Mrs. Frank Cabot's garden in Quebec give wind protection for pollinating insects as well as for tender young vegetable growth.

4. **Accessibility:**
   a. Proximity to the kitchen assures a minimum break in the food chain that extends from garden to kitchen to dining table (and, for the leftovers, back to the garden via the compost heap). This is vital to obtain maximum value from garden produce. Sweet corn, for example, tastes best if it is picked only when the water is already boiling on the stove. Last-minute additions or garnishes to a salad—marigold or sage flowers, young radish or beetroot leaves—are easily gathered.
   b. Proximity to the house also provides the opportunity to use the house walls as a support for training fruit trees. Pear, peach, and apple trees will flourish on a south-fac-

ing wall, and gooseberry or morello cherry will do well on a north- or east-facing wall.
   c. Proximity to the house allows the rainwater flowing off the roof to be used by draining the gutter into a water barrel or butt, where it can be stored for use in the summer.

5. **Wind protection:**
Wind inhibits the pollinating insects vital for production of fruit. It damages tender new growth of fruits and vegetables, and it causes ripening fruit to fall prematurely.

The ideal site is one that is naturally sheltered, but not so sheltered that the air becomes stagnant, which would be particularly bad for crops such as brussels sprouts, cabbages, and rutabagas. If natural shelter is not available, it can be created with walls, fences, or trees, as described in the next section. (If vegetables, particularly salads, are sheltered from even light winds, their yields will be increased by up to 50 percent.)

6. Frost protection:

Fruit is particularly susceptible to spoilage by frost at blossom time.

    a. Avoid selecting a low-lying site. Frost, like water, always runs downhill and lodges at the lowest point, creating a frost hollow.

    b. Avoid making a windbreak at the lowest point of the kitchen garden, as it will act as a frost barrier. If it is vital to have such a windbreak, cut a narrow opening at the lowest end. This will be sufficient to let the frosty air flow out without letting too much wind in.

If a kitchen garden must be created in a frost hollow, all is not lost:

    a. It is possible to choose only late-flowering or frost-tolerant fruit varieties.

    b. You can place the larger fruit varieties at the bottom of the garden, where, with luck, the frost will sink below the level of the flowers; place the smaller varieties on higher ground.

Lady Rothschild's old walled garden has been divided by hedges into units of more compact and manageable size.

7. Site size:

Kitchen garden plots will, of course, vary in size depending on availability of space and individual requirements, but the following guidelines indicate what can be expected from plots of different sizes:

100–150 square feet (10 x 10 or 10 x 15 feet): This small size will provide salads and tomatoes for a four-person family for many months of the year.

200–250 square feet (10 x 20 or 10 x 25 feet): Beans, onions, one or more kinds of fruit, and other money-saving crops may be added.

Above: The Chapelle garden in the wine country of northern California is open at the lower end to let cold air drain out.

Opposite: The ordered beds of Villandry in France are a study in kitchen garden design. Note the use of edgings to contrast color and the use of fruit trees to add height.

600 square feet (20 x 30 feet): This is sufficient for a full-sized domestic kitchen garden.

800 square feet (20 x 40 feet): Add main crop potatoes.

For centuries, vegetables have been grown in Asia in the "bed system": narrow beds worked from the adjoining paths and kept fertile by the constant application of layers of manure or compost. In Europe, vegetables were grown in the same way until the advent of the horse-drawn hoe, which resulted in the development of the "field system." In the field system, vegetables are grown efficiently in long rows, but, unfortunately, the soil structure between the rows can become broken down as a result of the frequent use of these paths for the processes of cultivation—digging, manuring, weeding, thinning—and cropping. When the use of the field system—ideal for large-scale estate and commercial production—became widespread for the small domestic kitchen garden, it reduced its visual attraction and

Left: The traditional "field system" of growing vegetables in long rows is still in operation at the Chateau de Beauregard near Paris, France.

increased its heavy labor requirement. Until it was recently abandoned, the field system prevented the development of the kitchen garden into a modern garden capable of holding its own with more conventional forms of ornamental gardens.

The revival of the bed system in the Western world has once more made the kitchen garden an attractive option for everyone. Building up the soil with frequent mulch applications removes the back-breaking activity of constant digging and reduces the need for watering. Productivity is increased because roots can penetrate more deeply and plants can be spaced more closely, which also reduces the need for weeding.

The raised-bed and deep-bed systems are refinements of the standard bed system. In the raised-bed system, the soil level is deliberately built up above the surrounding ground level to increase growing space, to improve sunlight radiation or drainage conditions, and to give deeper soil levels over rock, or over concrete on a city site. In China, and in many parts

Top: A standard bed—6 feet wide.

Above: A raised bed—6 feet wide—can accommodate an extra row of vegetables.

of Switzerland and Germany, raised beds have long been used as a means of raising the productivity of a small garden.

The method of increasing sunlight radiation by raising beds, often on a slope, was well understood in old

Right: The "bed system," using small, compact beds, was reintroduced at the Chateau de Villandry in the Loire Valley, France, in 1914.

estate kitchen gardens. The National Trust garden at Trengwainton in Cornwall is renowned for its raised beds. Facing west and southwest, and built up to a steep angle of 45 degrees, the garden absorbs maximum warmth from low spring sunshine, producing excellent early crops. A recent experiment at the University of California–Davis showed that creating even a five-degree slope in a bed was equivalent to moving 30 miles south for the production of early or tender vegetables. The beds should be at least 12 inches high and they can be either flat- or round-topped.

Raised beds are an often-used device in city yards. On a site where rock is just underneath the surface, raised beds provide a soil depth sufficient to grow fruit and vegetables. In some cases, the beds can be raised even higher than illustrated behind dwarf retaining walls. In a small garden, these have added advantages: they deter children and dogs from crossing the beds, they supply extra seating in the garden if they are 15 to 18 inches high and comfortably wide, and, if they are at least 29 inches high, they make gar-

(continued on p. 31)

Above: If beds are restricted in size, as they are in M. and Mme. Adalbert de Bagneux's garden, La Coquetterie, in Normandy, they can be accessed without treading on and compacting the soil.

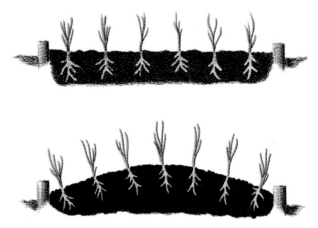

Center: A flat-topped bed.

Above: A round-topped bed is more efficient since more of the crop is angled toward the sun.

Sudborough Old Rectory,
Northamptonshire, England

MR. AND MRS. HUNTINGTON

In the kitchen garden at Sudborough Old Rectory, none of the vegetable beds are bigger than 7½ feet square, so it is possible to plant, tend, and harvest each from the surrounding paths. So convenient is this arrangement that the Huntingtons make no apologies for having their house guests give them a hand with the weeding.

The small size of these beds is also applauded by members of the Huntington family, who prefer not to have a tedious glut of one vegetable to be eaten up in one season. Not only are the beds small, but they are all the same size. This means less time spent coordinating plant rotation schemes. A scheme that works well in a bed one year can simply be transferred to an adjoining bed the next. The beds are arranged in groups of four, and each group is surrounded by narrower borders, creating a complete unit. One of these units (see illustration on page 29) would make a perfect plan for a kitchen garden on a small plot, and units can be combined for larger plots. The Old Rectory garden incorporates no fewer than six of these units.

The way the beds have been planted with vegetables to make interesting designs warrants careful study. In many, a checkerboard pattern is created with alternate blocks of vegetables of contrasting colors—white with ruby chard, or green with purple cabbage, for example. Checkerboard patterns are also made with vegetables of contrasting form. For example, blocks of tall sweet corn are planted alternately with blocks of dwarf lettuce. Triangular

Left: The garden's matrix of 7½-foot-square beds is convenient for planting, maintenance, and cropping.

Below: A pair of standard *Salix alba* 'Hakura Mishuka' (a dwarf Japanese willow variety) establish a change of color key.

patterns are used in other beds. Diagonal lines of purple orach, purple-sprouting broccoli, purple lettuce, and red kohlrabi divide the square beds into triangles, which are then planted with contrasting green vegetables.

The Huntingtons have placed great emphasis on giving a sense of height to the design. They planted a clipped cone or corkscrew of box at each corner of every bed. (These were imported from a nursery in Italy and took some time to settle down in the harsh-er English climate.) Standard roses, standard goose-berries, and standard *Salix alba* 'Hakura Mishuka' (a dwarf willow variety from Japan with green, cream, and pink variegated foliage), all about 5 feet high, are disposed in many of the beds. Others boast 'Victoria' plums trained into 7-foot-high festoons.

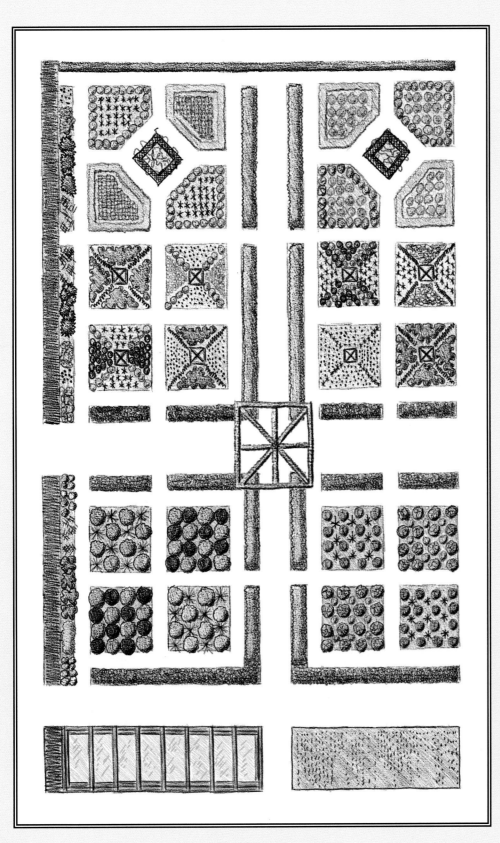

Left: A plan of the garden at Sudborough Old Rectory.

Opposite: The large trumpet flower of a squash growing on one of the garden's arbors.

Some of the paths are spanned by iron arches, also 7 feet high, which support rambling roses. The center of the garden is marked by a great domed arbor, 15 feet high and also in iron.

Any of these features might be used in smaller gardens. However, standard plants should be used sparingly, as they do have disadvantages. Their foliage casts shadows over vegetables, and their root systems compete for nutrients in the soil and make digging and planting difficult. In addition, their canopy of foliage needs pruning, training, and regular spraying with water.

Two final tips for planning a kitchen garden can be gleaned at Sudborough Old Rectory. First, because the foliage of most vegetables is in the cooler tones of green, purple, or blue, choose a material for the garden paths that is contrastingly warm in tone. The Huntingtons chose concrete paving slabs and bricks in a warm terra-cotta color. As with many colored concrete surfaces, the initially overbright color has now faded to a dusty, quieter pink. Second, how do you resolve the dilemma of the many edible plants whose beautiful flowers are never appreciated because the plants are cropped before the flowers open? The Huntingtons solution is to let a plant like chicory, for example, flower in alternate years, eating its foliage in the years between.

It is now six years since the kitchen garden at Sudborough was laid out with advice, in the initial stages, from Rosemary Verey. It is a source of constant delight and fulfillment to its owners. It looks best in high summer when potted orange and olive trees are taken from the greenhouse and set out along the paths to give the garden a festive air. There they are joined by blueberries grown in smaller pots filled with acid soil. As an American, Mrs. Huntington feels that fresh blueberries are indispensable in this garden.

Left: The kitchen garden at La Petite Fontanille, Provence, France, demonstrates that beds need not be simple rectangles or squares but can be circular, triangular, or hexagonal, as desired.

Below: In Ryan Gainey's garden in Atlanta, Georgia, the beds are laid out on a diagonal line to improve the orientation of the vegetables toward the sun.

dening convenient for elderly or physically handicapped people. In fact, gardening at this height will halve the strain and double the pleasure for everyone who pulls a weed or plucks a head of lettuce.

The deep bed system is also useful where the soil is sufficiently deep but deficient in nutrients. During the initial preparation of the beds, the ground is dug two spits, or spadefuls, deep; the bottom spit is enriched with organic manure during the process.

BED SIZE

The bed system of growing vegetables requires that the beds be narrow enough that, when worked from both sides, the entire area can be reached without stepping on and compacting the soil. This can be achieved by making no bed more than 5 feet wide. In most modern kitchen gardens, the width varies, between 3 and 5 feet, only occasionally reaching 6 or 7 feet, depending on personal preference. There is no similar restriction on the bed length. It is purely a matter of convenience not to have beds that are too long, as walking or wheeling a barrow around them becomes a nuisance. Therefore, it is better to restrict them to 10 or 12 feet in length. It is easier to

arrange crop rotation with small, narrow beds, and to plan each bed with a single, or at most, a double, crop at any one time.

The size of today's standard seed packet is usually based on the amount of seed required for a row 30 feet in length. The same amount can be spread over five rows, each 6 feet in length—in fact, just the amount required for a small, narrow bed.

BED SHAPE

Even though a repetitive arrangement of small beds constitutes the ideal domestic kitchen garden layout, the beds do not need to be in simple rectangles or squares. Circles, triangle, hexagons, or other geometric figures can all be used successfully. Surprisingly, a hexagon is a more efficient shape for planting than a square.

Although chores, such as sowing, staking, and hoeing, are easier in beds of regular shape, beds of irregular shape—for example, wider at one end than the other—can be managed by using slow-growing crops like brassicas or leeks at the wide end and fast-maturing crops such as lettuces, radishes, and shallots at the narrow end. Further, there is no reason why curved or serpentine beds should not be both practical and attractive. Nor is there any reason why vegetables should not be grown in a border in the same way that flowers are grown in a perennial border. In fact, Gertrude Jekyll suggested growing vegetables to make a "beautiful bit of summer gardening." She recommended using gourds, squashes, and runner beans as climbers; rhubarb, globe artichokes, and sea kale for beauty of shape and foliage; and tufts of horseradish for its handsome, deep green leaves. Be wary, however, of making the overall layout of the garden too complicated: it may become inefficient if activities like barrowing or trailing a hose are too difficult.

BED ORIENTATION

Although the arrangements of vegetable beds are determined finally by factors of construction and

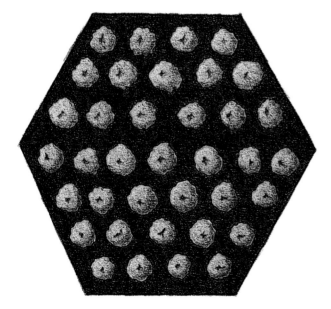

A hexagonal bed with no wasted planting area.

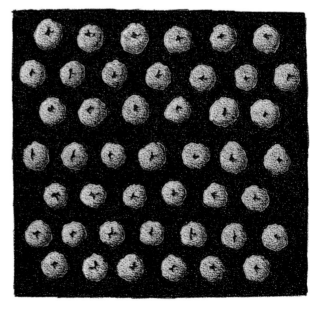

A square bed with wasted edge area.

aesthetics, it is worth remembering that certain orientations are inherently better than others. In theory, beds for summer crops are best aligned on a north–south axis, so that both sides get an equal amount of sun. On the other hand, beds for spring and autumn crops should have an east–west axis, so that their long sides have the maximum presentation to the lower, slanting sun. In practice, it is rarely possible to satisfy all such demands. It is simpler, usually, to align all beds on a north–south axis. The only exceptions to this rule are (1) on a sloping site, where the need to prevent soil erosion by planting across the slope is paramount, (2) in a garden exposed to westerly winds, where the need to align beds on an east–west axis to let the wind filter through the vegetable rows takes precedence, and (3) if the beds, for some reason, must be unusually long, in which case the rows may have to be at right angles to the path for convenience of access irrespective of their orientation. If, for any of these reasons, your beds end up with an east–west axis, plant the tall or climbing crops on the north side of the garden or bed, so that the shorter crops will still have access to summer sun.

BED LOCATION

It is helpful to locate some beds as near to the house as possible. Herb and salad beds, for example, should be easily accessible from the kitchen, so that quick forays may be made for garnishes during meal preparation. Likewise, winter crops like cabbages and brussels sprouts should be close to the house, or at least to a main path, for ease of gathering in bad weather.

SPECIAL BEDS

Because most vegetables are annuals, which require frequent sowing, cropping, and rotating, their location within the garden may change from year to year.

There are, however, a few vegetables that are perennials and so require a permanent spot in the garden, as do most kinds of fruit.

Perennial Vegetable Beds

Rhubarb, Jerusalem and globe artichokes, asparagus, horseradish, sorrel, perennial broccoli, and wild spinach will all occupy the same ground for a number of years (in the case of rhubarb and asparagus, for up to twenty years). It is best to plant them in the garden's peripheral beds, where they can remain undisturbed by the constant activity in the more centrally placed annual beds.

Fruit Beds

Trained fruit trees and fruit bushes—with the exception of strawberries—are semipermanent, lasting up to 10 or 15 years in the garden. They will, therefore, benefit from a separate bed that might even be strategically located so that their height can be used to screen a compost heap, garden shed, or frame.

Tall Annual Vegetable Beds

Sweet corn and climbing vegetables such as peas and beans are best confined to one or two beds on the north side of the garden. Otherwise, they will shade and thereby slow the growth of shorter vegetables.

Seed Beds

A special seed bed is necessary only if your intention is to raise vegetables in the old-fashioned way. Traditionally, vegetables, especially brassicas, were started in a seed bed and were transplanted to permanent positions when they were several inches high. This was done to save space, as the ground they would eventually occupy could be used for another crop in the meantime. The disadvantage of this system was that the roots of the plants were likely to be damaged during transplanting. The traditional seed

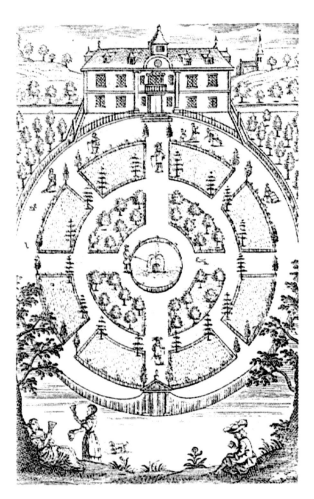

the design for their kitchen garden at Villandry on engravings in *Les Plus Excellents Bastiments de France,* published by Jacques Androuet du Cerceau in 1578–1579. Much later, Rosemary Verey was inspired by an illustration in Leonard Meager's *The New Arte of Gardening* (1697), to make her plan for the kitchen garden at Barnsley. There remain many fascinating plans in ancient gardening books waiting to inspire the designers of future kitchen gardens. The plan in John Worlidge's *Systema Horti-culturae* or *The Art of Gardening* (1677), for example seems very appropriate for such an adaptation.

Ideas from Art History

European paintings, particularly those from the sixteenth and seventeenth centuries, often show small gardens as the background of a portrait or as part of a broader landscape. Utens's late-sixteenth-century views of Florentine gardens, for example, contain innumerable ideas that could be adapted for use in a modern garden.

bed has been largely abandoned in favor of raising young plants in individual containers in plastic or polystyrene trays, in a greenhouse or a frame. Transplanting the plant in its own soil gives it an added advantage.

BED ARRANGEMENT AND DESIGN

A modern kitchen garden requires an overall design based on a repeat pattern of small beds, so that annual vegetable crops can be easily rotated from one bed to the other in successive years. In devising such a design, there are many useful ideas to be found in unexpected places—in the pages of garden history or on the canvasses of famous painters, for example.

Ideas from Garden History

The ideas for the design of two outstanding modern kitchen gardens came from plans seen in antique gardening books. Joachim and Ann Carvalho based

Islamic Art as a Source of Ideas

For religious reasons, the art of Islam was forbidden to represent the human figure. Instead, elaborate abstract patterns, which are best seen in their carpets and tilework, were developed. Many of these designs can be adapted as the basis for some intriguing garden plans.

Modern Art as a Source of Ideas

Modern art, like Islamic art, depends on the power of abstract patterns for effects. A careful study of these can furnish interesting ideas for unusual kitchen garden plans. An obvious example is the work of the early twentieth-century Dutch painter, Piet Mondrian.

When devising a pattern, make sure a focal point is incorporated. You may omit the vegetables in one of the beds and substitute some architectural or sculptural feature; a piece of topiary or another plant of eye-catching form or foliage is effective. In any case, the focal feature should not cast too much

Above: A plan for a kitchen garden based on an Utens painting.

Right: A modern kitchen garden plan based on an Islamic tile design.

shadow on the beds around it. A column or an obelisk, whether stone, trellis, or topiary, makes an ideal subject. It provides height, often the missing element in vegetable gardens, and its narrowness will not cast excessive shade. If a more substantial focal point is desired, then it should be of light, skeletal construction. A trellis of wood or iron will cast only dappled shade.

A more substantial structure (such as the summer house at Stavordale Priory) should be placed on the north side of the garden, so that it will not cast heavy shade over the growing area. Some gardens might benefit from a pair of focal features, at each end for example, rather than a single central one. Other designs, particularly the modern ones, may be best suited by a focal point that is off-center rather than central to the design.

PATHS

The paths between beds are part of a garden's architecture, defining people's movements and resting places. But they also give the garden its basic visual

remainder of the paths can be 18 inches wide. In a small garden, all of the paths can be this width, or some subsidiary paths can be 12 inches wide, the narrowest practical width. In a very small garden, where any paths might seem wasteful, they can be eliminated by using stepping stones to give a solid foothold from which to work and harvest the vegetables in wet weather. The stepping stones can be placed in either formal or informal patterns, giving the garden visual structure as well as practicality.

and spatial structure, guiding the eye as much as the feet. In addition to providing pleasing patterns, the paths must provide easy access to such important functional locations as the tool shed, a greenhouse or frame, the compost or manure heap, and, most important, the kitchen. After all, the true *raison d'être* of the kitchen garden is lost if it is not closely located to the kitchen.

Hygiene dictates that the paths should be designed to be easily hosed or swept clean. They should be firm enough to take a lot of wear and well-drained enough to ensure that feet stay dry. Water flows quickly off hard paving if it is laid with a slight camber—that is, a slope from the center to both sides.

Path widths can vary according to the size of the garden. In a very large garden, a main path 4 to 5 feet wide will allow two people to pass each other or walk side-by-side in comfort. A medium-sized garden might have a main path $2\frac{1}{2}$ feet wide to allow for occasional hauling of wide barrow loads. The

Right: A kitchen garden plan based on Piet Mondrian's painting style.

Opposite: At St. Mary's Farm, in Lady Mary Keen's garden in Berkshire, England, a free-draining gravel path leads the eye through a pear arch to the flowering clump of rhubarb beyond.

Path Materials

The choice of paving materials should be dictated not only by aesthetic considerations, but also by climate. A rainy climate, for example, demands an easily drained surface like gravel, paving with open or porous joints, or concrete with a definite slope from the center of the path to both sides to assist in run-off. A snowy climate requires a surface that is smooth rather than textured, so that snow can be removed without it lodging in the crevices. Paving materials should reflect the character of adjacent buildings and the surrounding landscape, and their size should be scaled to the size of the garden. Redwood decking is at home in California, granite or brick in the eastern United States, and stone in

Right: At Sudborough Old Rectory, Northamptonshire, England, concrete paving can be easily hosed and swept clean—hygiene is important because the produce of a kitchen garden is eaten.

Left: At the Old Rectory, Mrs. Ralph Merton's garden at Burghfield, Berkshire, England, a grass path needs regular mowing and edging, yet is cool to look at and comfortable to walk on.

the English Cotswolds. Combinations of different materials can give a handsome patterned effect, but the composition should be restrained, as busy patterns distract the eye from a harmonious plan and planting.

Grass

Although this is a cheap form of path surface, grass paths through the garden need to be numerous and wide to avoid excessive wear on this soft, growing material. It is really suitable only for larger kitchen gardens like Criqueboeuf in France or Les Quatre Vents in Canada. Grass is cool and green to look at, and silent and soft to walk on, but it is highly labor-intensive, needing to be mown and edged regularly. As with gravel, neat and tidy gardening is required, as it is difficult to clean off dirt or muck spilled from a wheelbarrow.

Concrete

Poured as a continuous path surface, concrete has the reputation of being dull in appearance, but, in its defense, it has suffered from much unimaginative use. There are many possible ways of enlivening its appearance; the most obvious is by brushing it as it dries to bring the gravel in the mix to the surface. This is called an *exposed aggregate finish* and it results

At St. Mary's Farm, a brick path is appropriate in a setting of brick walls and buildings.

in an attractively textured surface. A concrete path's appearance can also be enhanced by taking advantage of the expansion joints placed every 8 to 10 feet along its length to prevent cracking. A contrasting material—a line of bricks, granite setts, slate, concrete slabs, or even wood—can be inserted at the joints to create an interesting rhythmical pattern. Concrete's advantages are that it is long-lasting and efficient, with a minimum number of joints to get a barrow's wheels stuck or to harbor unwelcome insect pests. Occasional sweeping or hosing will keep it clean, and an annual watering with simazine will keep it weed free.

Brick

As expensive to buy and lay as stone, brick is most appropriate in a setting of brick walls and buildings. Of all pavings, it is the warmest in color, the easiest to walk on (even with bare feet in hot weather), and the finest in scale, and it offers the widest variety of interesting patterns. (Remember, the more complex the pattern, the more expensive it is to lay.) Other materials—flagstones, cobbles, or setts—can be interwoven or placed as an edging to give further interesting variations on brick path design. Such a mixture of materials is especially appropriate when the

house is faced with a similar mixture. For example, a brick house may have stone windowsills and lintels, or ornaments in a contrasting brick color. The cue for the garden design can be taken from the house design and thus give a remarkable effect of unity.

The disadvantage of bricks is that only hard-fired engineering or facing bricks will withstand frost without splitting. Hard paving bricks are manufactured for stable or industrial flooring and come in a variety of good colors, including heather, black, and dark blue. (Those at Barnsley House came from the floor of a disused blacksmith's forge).

Gravel

Gravel comes in two forms, natural and man-made. The latter comes in two types, binding gravel and graded gravel. *Binding gravel* is obtained by crushing rocks into a powder, which forms a cementing medium. After it is watered and rolled, it becomes a firm surface that is extremely durable. Granite dust and Breedon gravel are materials commonly used for making a binding gravel. A variety of binding gravel is called *hoggin*: sand, silt, and clay are added to the powdered stone to increase binding. Although it provides a practical surface in a utility area, it tends to tread up in wet weather and turns dusty in dry

Left: Antique bricks and smooth slate squares are interwoven to make a strong pattern in the Lufkin garden in Lakeville, Connecticut.

Opposite: Plants often drape over the tightly kept box hedge at Villandry, France.

weather. *Graded gravel* is composed of rock chippings passed through a mesh with openings that can vary from ¼ to ¾ inch square, depending on how fine a gravel is required. A ¼-inch mesh is used to get fine material known as pea gravel. This gives a sophisticated, formal look, but it needs frequent raking to keep it tidy and in place. A ½-inch gravel mesh produces a more practical surface: it is heavy enough to stay in place and yet not so rough that it destroys shoes or furniture placed on it. The chippings are sharp-sided, because they have not been weathered or waterworn over as long a period as river shingle, for example. However, it is just these sharp, angular facets that make the chips interlock tightly, resulting in a surface that is cleaner and more likely to stay in place than binding gravel.

Natural gravel or shingle is dredged from a riverbed, where tiny pebbles are worn smooth by the

Right: Brick as a paving material offers the widest scope for making interesting patterns, as demonstrated in the garden of Barnsley House, England.

fixed along the path sides to contain the loose material, and the gravel must be spread on a well-rolled and compacted foundation of larger stones. Even with this preparation, the surface may be too soft to easily roll a wheelbarrow on. The solution is a narrow strip of hard paving down the center of the path that will both support the barrow wheel and provide an interesting paving detail. The general maintenance of gravel paths is quite easy. They require only occasional hosing down to take off the accumulation of dust that adheres to the chippings, and an

action of water. Because of its smoothness, it is preferable to the man-made gravels in places where children are likely to play.

Gravels come in as many different colors as there are rock faces. Some are of a single, uniform color. Others are variegated, with colors ranging from dark to light, gray to brown and shades of white.

Although gravel is the cheapest surfacing material, particularly if produced locally, its proper installation can be expensive. An edging board must be

annual watering with a weedkiller like simazine. For high-quality maintenance, however, they should be regularly raked level and smooth. The disadvantage of gravel is that it is difficult to keep clean, especially if the gardener is untidy and frequently spills soil onto it while digging or dressing the beds. The problem of dirt being carried into the house on the soles of shoes can be alleviated by laying a stretch of hard paving material between the gravel paths and the house entry. Remember also that gravel is not a

(continued on p. 47)

Les Quatre Vents, Quebec, Canada

MR. AND MRS. FRANK CABOT

The edges of vegetable beds become a critical consideration when a kitchen garden is laid out on a sloping site. They then function also as retaining walls that maintain the level of soil in the beds. At Les Quatre Vents, the beds are edged and retained by walls of 6-inch-square, treated spruce logs from British Columbia. This versatile material is also used to form the steps along the paths and to stake the tomatoes, beans, and sweet peas in the beds, thus giving the garden an underlying aesthetic unity. The hard line of the timber walls

Above: On the falling ground, timber edges become dwarf walls to retain the levels within the vegetable beds.

Left: An intricate pattern of bed shapes and sizes has been conceived to suit the steeply sloping contours of the site.

is softened by an inner line of dwarf marigolds, planted each year by Mrs. Cabot with seed saved from the
previous year's planting. The saved seed ensures
a delightful variety of
form and color—one
that could not be ob-
tained from a commer-
cial packet of seed, which
usually results in a prosa-
ic uniformity of habit and
flower color. In a similar
way, the hard line of the
timber steps is softened
by allowing feverfew, with
its daisylike flowers, to
seed itself in the con-
struction joints.

A significant advan-
tage of the timber edging
system is that it is capable
of being adapted to suit a
rapidly changing, round
contour. At Les Quatre
Vents, for example, no
two of the nine vegetable
beds are the same—
some beds have up to

four different levels. The
timber edging can be
cut or added to, and
increased or decreased
in height, as circum-
stances require. Also, it
is an edging system that
does not harken back to any particular antique style
of design. Les Quatre Vents is the only garden featured here that is uncompromisingly modern, with
a layout derived solely from the practical necessities
of vegetable gardening and the contours of the site.
This does not mean it is a garden without sentiment
or humor. Its scarecrows, for example, are raffishly
dressed in the Cabots' old clothes.

Les Quatre Vents, lying as it does under a thick
blanket of snow for much of the winter, has the most
severe climate of any of the gardens described here.
With the exception of a few brussels sprouts grown
for the Christmas festival, this is a summer garden.
Seedlings are planted out in May and the harvest is

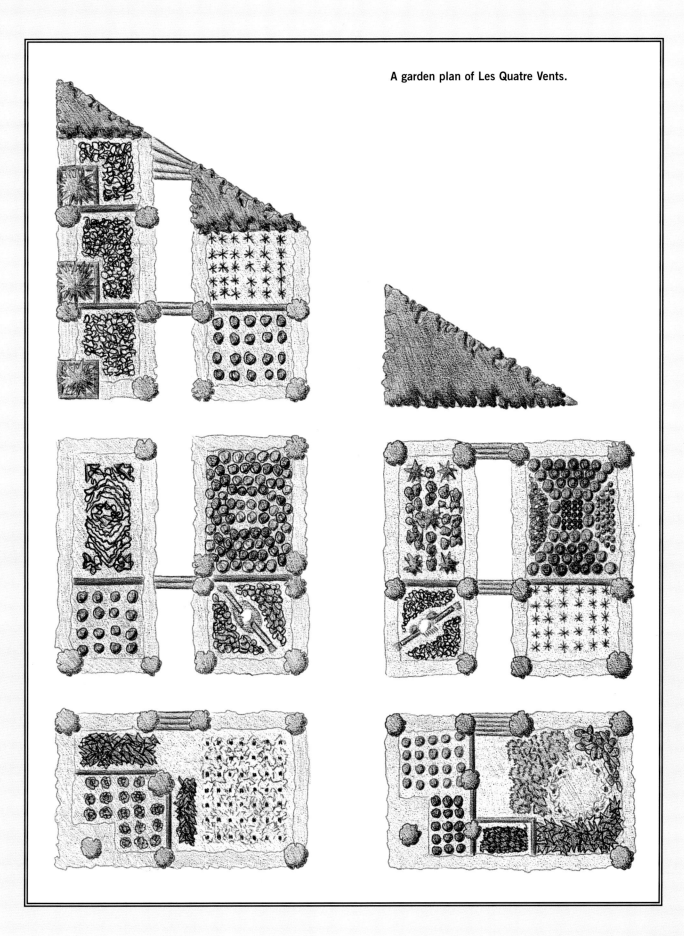

A garden plan of Les Quatre Vents.

completed by mid October. The annual routine begins each year with the arrival of the season's seed catalogs before Christmas. (Stokes' catalog, with business in both the United States and Canada, is the most useful, because it specializes in very hardy vegetable varieties.) During the more relaxed moments of the Christmas holiday, Mrs. Cabot plans on paper the next year's planting. After the ordered seeds have arrived, they are sown in the greenhouse by the Cabots' gardener, a year-round resident in Quebec. When the Cabots arrive from New York in May, the seedlings are planted out and the gardening begins.

As the hard climate is particularly good for growing brassicas, great attention is paid to the 20-foot-square brassica bed. Broccoli, kale, brussels sprouts, kohlrabi, and green cabbage are planted in a series of bands radiating from the center, and the overall design is bisected in both directions by diagonal lines of contrasting purple cabbage. To keep the bed luxuriant with foliage at all times, successions of crops are planned; for example, early cauliflowers are interplanted with late sprouts, early cabbages with late kohlrabi, and the broccoli varieties chosen are those that send up new heads after the first have been cut.

The squash bed boasts a central circlet of 2-foot-high staked tomatoes (grown in patent water-encased containers plunged into the ground to reduce frost damage to the roots). Around them trail the handsomely foliaged summer squashes, cucumbers, and other squashes. The result is a rampant and intertwining growth that creates an almost subtropical look, in complete contrast to the tightly bunched cabbage heads in the adjoining bed. Other beds are devoted to root crops, potatoes, sweet corn, or strawberries, but the garden is not restricted to fruit and vegetables. Delphiniums, Shasta daisies, chrysanthemums, and tobacco flowers, supported on cat's cradles of twine and bamboo canes, add their bright colors to the muted tones of the surrounding vegetables.

Although a full range of standard vegetables and fruits are grown at Les Quatre Vents, the Cabots are always keen to introduce new edible plants to their garden. On a plant-hunting expedition to Nepal, they noticed that the pods of a plant called *Cyclanthera pedata* 'Edulis', which clambered all over the village houses, were a staple in the local diet. They collected seed from it and now grow it in their own garden. The Cabots, and gardeners like them, are pioneers who bring about advances both in gardening and in garden design.

suitable material for a sloping site, because it is a loose material and it will eventually end up at the lowest point.

Stone

Together with brick, this is the most attractive path surface, but it is expensive to buy and to lay. The material's natural irregularities provide a rich, textural quality that can never be achieved with concrete. However, it is essential to select pieces that fit in an informal pattern, rather than to cut them, which does not produce a natural effect. Old York stone, for example, is traditionally laid in informal rings around a series of centrally placed keystones. "Crazy paving" was very fashionable in the first half of this century, but it was rarely done well because it took patience to fit the broken pieces of old stone neatly, if haphazardly, together. More often, ill-fitting arrangements of large stones were filled in with smaller, gap-filling pieces to make a poorly laid and short-lived product. Granite paving (often called Belgian blocks) is frequently used in continental Europe. The blocks are approximately the size of brick, but square. They were originally intended for street paving and were placed so that a horse might gain a foothold between the joints. They are excellent in granite areas where their somber gray blends with walls of local stone. The cheapest form of paving stone is reconstituted stone. In size and shape similar to concrete paving, it is made of stone dust; it retains its color and weathers as attractively as real stone.

Concrete Paving

The cheapest paving material by far, this comes in slabs with a variety of sizes and shapes, including rectangular, square, round, and hexagonal. Many are artificially tinted, and their color fades (a blessing in some cases, as the colors are often garish to start with). Usually, the dark colors lighten and the light colors darken from accumulations of dirt as well as from natural fading. When selecting a slab for a particular location, look at it both wet and dry, as the color changes markedly from one condition to the other. For a small garden, select a small-sized slab of simple design; it will show off the planting to better advantage than one of fancy design with brightly colored pointing. The smooth-faced slabs are easier to keep clean by sweeping and hosing than those with deeply indented patterns in which dirt lodges.

EDGES

Serious thought needs to be given to the edges of the beds in a vegetable garden. A consequence of frequent top-dressings is the alternate rising and falling of the soil level as mulch is added and then settles and is absorbed. A hard or, even better, a raised edge will prevent the soil from spilling over onto the paths during this process. A stone edging looks particularly nice when setting off a grass or gravel path. If the edging is raised, it will also give a firm, crisp edge to the beds. Such a curb will emphasize a design that might otherwise be obliterated eventually by the planting. It will also underline the design in winter, when many of the beds may lie fallow. Hard edgings of brick, stone, or concrete

Left: At La Petite
Fontanille, in Provence,
France, the warm tones
of the terra-cotta tile
edgings complement the
cool greens of the Swiss
chard.

Right: Nancy McCabe's
collection of antique scallop-
shaped moldings make refined
bed edgings in her garden in
Falls Village, Connecticut.
Although the individual
pieces match approximately
in size, they vary in their
impressed patterns.

Left: : Terra-cotta edgings in
the traditional rope-molding
pattern are used in Mrs.
Bunny Williams's
Connecticut garden.

Right: Sawn spruce logs
from British Columbia make
no-nonsense bed edgings at
Les Quatre Vents, Quebec.

sometimes look too harsh in a domestic setting. If this is the case, formal or dwarf hedges will give a softer effect. However, there is no reason why a variety of edgings might not be used in one garden, as Barnsley House does to magnificent effect.

Tiles, Bricks, or Timber

These will give a very neat effect, although there is always a risk of pests harboring in the tile or brick joints and under the timber. Untreated larch, birch, or pine logs make an informal rustic edging, appropriate for beds in a woodland setting.

Box

Buxus sempervirens is the most widely used and traditional of all bed edgings. Its use was first advocated by the great French vegetable gardeners of the eighteenth century for its value in giving shelter to beds of young seedlings. The variety 'Suffruticosa' is most valued because of its neat, dwarf habit and fine foliage. With persistent clipping, it can be kept as low as a few inches high. If left to its own devices, it will reach 4 or 5 feet in height. Expensive to buy, it also drains the soil of nutrients and harbors slugs. These problems can be controlled by plentiful feeding and

the application of slug bait. Otherwise, box needs little maintenance except for a biennial clipping.

Herbs

The best low-growing herbs to use for productive edgings are chives, thyme, parsley, dwarf hyssop, wall germander, winter savory, and alpine strawberries. They require more attention than box, as they need regular division, replacement, or seed-sowing. The colors of the edges can be chosen to suit beds with planned color schemes. For example, golden thyme or sage makes a striking edging for a bed devoted exclusively to fruits and vegetables with a golden color. Purple sage will match a purple color scheme; lavender, a silver one. For taller, space-dividing hedges within the garden, lavender, southernwood, and the upright rosemary are suitable.

Grass

A grass edging furnishes the best base for setting off plant colors and textures. However, if it is too narrow, it will be difficult to mow and the edges will crumble. It is therefore truly suitable only in a large garden, where sufficient space is available.

Walls, Fences, and Hedges

From both a practical and an aesthetic point of view, a kitchen garden needs to be enclosed. A boundary wall, fence, or hedge provides shelter from the wind, excludes animal and human intruders, gives privacy, and, if necessary, tempers near-by traffic or other noises. While improving the garden's microclimate, the boundary also provides a visual frame, thus establishing the garden's setting. What kind of boundary is best? This depends on the garden's setting, the architectural style of the house, and the gardener's preferences for various climbing vegetables and fruit.

If the garden site is naturally sheltered and the views from it are appealing, an open fence will complement rather than compete with the surrounding landscape. However, if the view beyond the garden is unattractive, it is better to surround it with high walls or hedges and design an inwardly oriented garden focused on one or two central, eye-catching features. Sometimes, a site offers a good view in one direction only; then, an open fence on that side is desirable, with high walls or hedges surrounding the other three sides. This situation can give rise to an interesting two-part design. The area next to the fence can have an arrangement of beds that allows the eye to focus on the view, and the remaining part can have a contrasting, inwardly focused design backed by high walls.

The second consideration in deciding how the garden should be enclosed is a practical one. A garden that is entirely surrounded by walls becomes a frost trap. Although this was not a cause for concern in the great kitchen gardens of old (which were often surrounded by 12-foot-high walls, and the area of the frost pocket was relatively insignificant), in a small garden such walls should be avoided. Allow for cold air to drain downward and out of the garden by erecting a perforated screen, such as an open-work gate, at the lowest level of the garden. Rather than resulting in awkwardness or disunity in the boundary design, this can provide a welcome variation to it. For example, one wall of perforated brick will perfectly match another three of solid brick if the finishes are similar.

The material to use in the boundary construction depends on two factors: (1) the environment external to the garden and (2) the architectural style of the house. The first involves choosing a material that is already in use in the surrounding neighborhood. This ensures that the new garden will fit in visually with its environment. As William Robinson wrote in *The English Flower Garden* (1883), "The best kind of garden should arise out of its site and conditions as happily as a primrose out of a cool bank." Thus, you may decide to use a brick wall, a yew hedge, or a stained timber fence because you have observed their use in the vicinity. Fitting the design to the architectural style of the house usually means repeating one of the materials used in the house. For example, brick is harmonious around a garden attached to a brick house, or white-painted wood fencing alongside a white-painted clapboard house, but brick garden walls look incongruous with a wooden house. Concrete walls or tubular metal fencing are unsuitable for a traditional house, but they look perfect with the clean lines of contemporary construction. Using the architectural style of the house to "prompt" the design details of the boundary can mean anything from designing an elaborately crafted fence with white-painted pickets and finials, to the simplest construction of palisade or split rail for the relaxed ambiance of a rural retreat.

The last factor to consider in the design is how effectively the boundary functions as a windbreak. This factor is important because vegetable yields improve up to 50 percent if protection from high winds is offered. An ideal windscreen is one that is half permeable: a solid windscreen blocks the wind instead of filtering it, causing local leeward turbulence and resultant damage to crops. A boundary wall provides wind protection for a distance of between six and ten times its height. For example, a 3-foot-high wall can be expected to shelter a garden 20 to 30 feet wide. A garden 40 to 60 feet wide needs a wind barrier at least 6 feet high. If the site is very exposed or subject to extreme wind speeds, it may be advisable to introduce some internal wind barriers in addition to the surrounding boundary barrier. This provides the opportunity to create small outdoor "rooms"—a particularly pleasant addition to any kitchen garden.

The house at Stavordale Priory, Somerset, England, is constructed of stone, making the choice of construction material for the kitchen garden walls an easy one.

1. STONE

Although expensive, stone is a natural complement to plants in many rural areas, and its use in garden walls heightens the sense of the garden being part of the natural scene. A dry-stone wall—one that has no mortar joints but relies on gravity and the method of construction for stability—may look appealing in the landscape, but it is unfortunately impractical for a kitchen garden where mortar joints are needed to hold the ties for training fruit against the wall. (Any intention to build one over 3 feet high should involve the advice of an expert.) However, a south-facing stone wall is an ideal surface for growing a fan-trained nectarine, apricot, or peach. An east- or

west-facing wall is good for loganberries, blackberries, or a fan-trained plum, and a north-facing wall will suit a morello cherry. Although a south-facing wall is the most valuable because fruit grown on it will be larger and better-flavored as a result of ripening in the sun, the other walls contribute by providing later-ripening fruit and so extending the eating season. In deciding the height of the wall, it is useful to know the height required for growing different kinds of wall-fruit. On walls up to 6 feet in height, dwarf apples and pears can be espaliered, and gooseberries, red or white currants, blackberries, and raspberries can be cordon- or fan-trained. Walls from 6 to 8 feet high are required for cordons, fans, or multiple-tier espaliers of apples or pears on semidwarf rootstock. A height of at least 7 feet is needed for training most stone fruits (apricots, nectarines, peaches, plums, greengages, and morello cherries) and at least 8 feet for the vigorous sweet cherry.

Left: The 12-foot-high brick walls of the old kitchen garden at the Chateau de Miromesnil, Normandy, France, match in color and scale the brick walls of the chateau itself.

Below: In Lakeville, Connecticut, the new garden walls are constructed with antique brick to give a settled, mellow look.

(continued on p. 59)

Lakeville, Connecticut, United States

Mrs. Elise Lufkin

Any mention of a walled kitchen garden brings to mind the great estate gardens of the past. Walls of a more modest size, however, can provide a practical way of enclosing a smaller kitchen garden today. A good example can be seen in Mrs. Lufkin's garden in Lakeville, Connecticut, designed by Nancy McCabe. Her garden (100 feet long by 40 feet wide) is surrounded by walls that are 6 feet high. Built of brick recycled from a demolition in Ohio, they are capped with the local blue limestone. Because a garden entirely surrounded by walls is a frost trap, an opening was made in

Above: Intermediate buttress walls divide the kitchen garden into a series of smaller, more sheltered areas.

Left: A cross view features the flowing hedges of the flowering catmint, *Nepeta* 'Six Hills Giant', lining the central path.

the lower end of the wall to let the frost drain out. This opening is filled with a latticework gate commissioned from the artist Christopher Hewat. A brick path runs down the center of the garden linking the three distinct, but not entirely separate, areas of the garden, which are divided by low buttress walls.

Above: A brick- and slate-paved sitting area is surrounded by beds of herbs, vegetables, and flowers, mixed in cottage garden style.

Right: Traditional cottage-garden edging plants—pinks, sweet williams, and parsley—frame the salad beds.

Opposite: Peaches enjoy basking in the heat reflected from warm brick walls.

The first area incorporates a brick-paved sitting area that is surrounded by mixed herb, vegetable, and flower beds. Old-fashioned, cottage-garden flowers—pinks, hollyhocks, cosmos, and columbines—are grown in rows between lettuce, cabbage, onions, and basil; on the walls behind, espaliered fruits alternate with buddleias like 'Nanhoe Blue' and 'White Profusion'. The presence of the buddleias ensures that the sitting area is alive with butterflies during the summer. To complete the design, clipped box balls punctuate the corners, and garden seats are based on a design by the English architect Sir Edwin Lutyens. As a finishing touch, glazed pots from Anduze in southern France are filled with the sweet-scented cherry pie or purple heliotrope, their violet flowers and bronze foliage set off to perfection by the pottery's glaze.

The central path is lined with a loose, flowing hedge of catmint, *Nepeta* 'Six Hills Giant', originally put in as tiny plants at one-foot centers. The sprays of lavender-colored flowers arch over the path for many weeks in early summer, after which they are cut back to produce a second flush in late summer or early autumn. The subsidiary paths are lined with traditional cottage-garden edgings—sweet williams, pinks, and parsley. The beds behind are also planted in a traditional cottage-garden fashion with smaller sunflowers, single dahlias, Japanese anemones, and lilies grown between rows of spinach, beans, and lettuce.

Mrs. Lufkin's garden is fascinating not only as a contemporary interpretation of the cottage garden, but also for its echoes of the traditional Italian *giardino segreto,* an enclosed private area within a much larger garden, usually directly accessible from the side of the house and used by the owner as a place of quiet, peaceful seclusion.

Stained timber fencing is characteristic of rural Connecticut, so the fencing in Mrs. Bunny Williams's garden is appropriate to its setting.

2. BRICK

Brick walls have a tailored look and, as a result, they are as expensive to build as stone walls. The cost is especially high if old bricks are used, as it is quite a task to clean them of old mortar and other debris for reuse. On the other hand, they have a mellow and settled look. Walls of new brick should be constructed with brick manufactured locally or with brick that has been traditionally used in the area. Quick visual "age" can be achieved by the disagreeable but effective method of painting the walls with liquid cow manure, which encourages the growth of mosses and lichens on the wall surface. The singular advantage of a brick wall is that it soaks up the maximum amount of the sun's heat and radiates it back slowly over a long period, thus gently ripening and flavoring the fruit growing on it. It was for this reason that the high walls of old estate kitchen gardens were often given an inner lining of brick. However, it is not necessary to have such high walls in a modern garden: the minimum heights required are the same as those given in the previous section. Many tender vegetables—tomatoes, peppers, eggplants, and sweet corn—will thrive basking in the reflected heat at the base of such a brick wall. If solid walls look too massive around a small garden, perforated or "honeycombed" walls can be used. Variety in design is achieved by varying the width of air spaces between the bricks, or by laying them at an angle to give a sawtooth pattern. For further informality, the brick can be combined with another material. For example, slate or flint could be incorporated, or the wall could be topped with wooden fencing.

A traditional white-painted picket fence atop a kitchen-garden wall at Mount Vernon, Virginia.

3. TIMBER

Although wood is the cheapest and easiest material available to make garden boundaries, it is also the most expensive to maintain. Annual examination is required to locate the problems of rotting and warping that consistently plague wood. Replacement of deteriorated sections and repainting, where necessary, must be done routinely. The worst problems can be avoided if (1) the top of the fence is protected with a heavy-duty timber capping and (2) the bottom of the fence is raised a few inches off the wet ground. (The resultant gap can be closed by a "gravel board," without interfering with the main fence.) A further disadvantage of timber fencing is that climbing plants can entwine themselves in the joints between the boards, causing warping as they grow. Timber, however, lends itself to the greatest variety of patterns, combinations, and colors. A timber wall can be constructed solid for complete privacy, partly open or louvered to give a light and airy effect, or mostly open to suggest a boundary rather than emphasize one. It can be very delicately designed, such as a beautifully crafted Japanese fence, or more utilitarian, such as a rough post-and-rail form. The fence's design should never overwhelm its sur-

roundings: if stained dark rather than painted white, it will appear to recede. Four to five feet is an adequate height for the timber wall of a small garden. Cedar, oak, or painted softwoods are the most common materials used.

Solid timber fences can be erected with boards that are butt-ended, lap-jointed, or interwoven, sawn or unsawn. The edges can be arranged either vertically or horizontally. The boards can be painted or treated with clear preservative to suit any architectural style. They can be bought in the form of prefabricated panels ready for fixing to posts that have already been set in the ground. Espaliered or cordoned fruit and many varieties of cane or bush fruit can be grown against them as they are grown against a stone wall.

Open timber fences are ideal for the very small garden as they let the sun through while tempering the wind. Ranch-style post-and-rail, in sawn oak, split chestnut, or painted softwood, is the most durable, but it can have too heavy an effect for a small garden. More delicate in design is traditional picket fencing, particularly suitable for older, rural locations. Its closely spaced timber and sawn tops make it dog- and child-proof, depending on its height. A

(continued on p. 64)

La Petite Fontanille, Provence, France

AMBASSADOR ANN COX CHAMBERS

If the site of a kitchen garden is naturally sheltered and its surroundings are attractive, an open fence rather than a solid wall of hedge may be an appropriate boundary. In the garden of La Petite Fontanille, the kitchen garden is surrounded by low, white-painted stud fencing that suggests rather than delineates enclosure.

The kitchen garden is, in fact, one of a matching pair of gardens: the other is an herb garden. Both are surrounded by low, white-painted, stud fencing

Ambassador Cox Chambers's garden is sheltered by trees on three sides, but the fourth is open to an extensive view of the surrounding plain.

Left: The garden is planted mainly with salad greens: lettuce and chicory in variety, as well as the chives shown here.

Below: The kitchen garden is one of a pair of matching gardens—the other is an herb garden.

of a character that is typically country American. In each garden, a path winds around a central roundel outside of which four beds fill the quarters of the garden's square. All of the beds are edged with dwarf lavender that spills out onto the pale Provençal gravel paths. Their sweet but pungent aroma lies heavily on the still summer air and encourages one to waste away the drowsy afternoon on one of the benches painted white to match the railings. In the kitchen garden, the beds are planted mainly with salads: let-

Left: Stone spheres, box balls, and clipped bays harmonize with the rounded shapes of the vegetable beds.

The design is based on a central roundel—a shape repeated in santolina in each of the bigger beds.

tuce in variety, chives, and chicory, but also spinach, onions, and leeks.

The tradition of kitchen gardening in Provence is recorded back to the Middle Ages. Documents from that period detail gardens in Aix-en-Provence, filled with cabbage, spinach, onions, leeks, pumpkins, and melons. Aromatic herbs and fruits, such as apples, pears, plums, cherries, peaches, and figs, together with walnuts and hazelnuts are mentioned. The fourteenth-century account books of the papal palace at Avignon give us a clear picture of such an early Provençal garden. La Petite Fontanille brings this ancient tradition of kitchen gardening up to date with a design by two of today's foremost designers, Rosemary Verey (whose own garden is described in this book) and Ryan Gainey from Atlanta (whose kitchen garden has frequently been photographed and described).

trelliswork fence also has a delicate air, but it is not suitable for growing espalier tree fruit or tough cane fruits such as raspberries and loganberries. It can, however, be ideal for growing climbing vegetables like peas, beans, or gourds. The major advantage of lattice is that its pattern remains to decorate the garden when the plants die down in winter. Also, it is an ideal support for plants growing in boxes on balconies or roof gardens. Post-and-wire is the cheapest form of open timber fencing (although it can be broken by adventurous children climbing on it). If the wire strands are strung every two feet, it makes a convenient support for soft fruit or low-espaliered tree fruit, and then it is a living, verdant screen from spring to autumn.

Timber fencing lends itself to some unusual and exciting variations:

1. "Junk" fencing, with materials like old telephone poles, railway ties, driftwood, and odd field stones, can combine to dramatic effect in a fence constructed with an artistic eye.

2. Split bamboo can be bought in rolls and fixed to vertical posts to give a fence inspired by Japanese design.

3. Chestnut or spit-cedar palings can also be bought in rolls and pinned to posts; this is often done to make fences in London's parks.

4. High, elegant, but temporary screens can be made with well-crafted osier, hazel, or reed hurdles. These are particularly useful within the garden, as they can be moved about when required to shelter young seedlings from wind and then stored away when not in use.

5. Similar movable screens, perhaps 1 to 2 feet high, can be made with fabric such as hessian, netting, or cheesecloth pinned to light timber frames that can be struck into the ground and moved as needed.

4. CONCRETE

A wall of concrete block is the cheapest form of solid, permanent enclosure. Its often rough finish can be made more presentable by plastering, painting, or masking with a thin veil of greenery. Cast concrete walls can work well with a house of contemporary architectural design; their bland, unobtrusive surfaces providing an excellent foil for eye-catching flowers and foliage. Virtually maintenance free, they can look too massive in a small garden. Concrete does have a more delicate, elegant expression, but this requires complex patterns too demanding visually to be restful in a small space. Concrete, therefore, should be used with special care in kitchen garden boundaries, and even then it is perhaps best in a setting of contemporary design.

5. IRON

Iron railings make the most sophisticated urban fences for a period town house, but they can look

At Te Doom, Ineke Greve's kitchen garden in Holland, the enclosing hedges are separated from the vegetable beds by a narrow path. Without it, their roots would compete for the available nutrients in the soil.

fussy and incongruous in other settings. Because of their design, they are usually unclimbable. They need regular maintenance. Second-hand or antique examples can often be purchased.

6. HEDGES

A hedge is often the right material to use in a kitchen garden boundary, especially in a rural setting. As is true for a wall or a fence, the hedging material should fit with the locality. A hedge of hornbeam, for example, will look appropriate in a neighborhood characterized by hornbeam trees. A hedge of randomly mixed materials, even native species, will blend well in a rural situation. A hedging material already in use in the neighborhood carries with it the assurance that it grows successfully in that particular soil and climate. The disadvantage of a hedge for a small garden is that it can act as a host for pests, diseases, and birds eager to consume the ripe produce. It can also compete with the crops for light and the available nutrients and moisture in the soil. Privet is especially greedy. However, this effect can be minimized by sinking a sheet of metal below soil level to contain the hedge's roots, or by designing a path along the base of the hedge to separate it from the crops.

An evergreen hedge, like a solid fence, is likely to block rather than filter the wind, causing leeward turbulence. A deciduous hedge forms a more effective windscreen, and beech and hornbeam make a substantial visual contribution to the garden (although, because they eventually reach a minimum of 3 feet in width, they are suitable only for larger gardens). Productive hedges of gooseberry, currant, or rosemary are suitable for intermediate shelter within the garden. Box, lavender, and sage make ideal miniature hedges around the vegetable beds, providing welcome shelter for young seedlings. Evergreen hedges also fulfill the important role of emphasizing the garden's pattern and design, even when many of the beds are partly or totally unplanted.

In Lady Rothschild's garden, high yew hedges provide internal intermediate shelter.

Last, informal windscreens can be made within the garden by using lines of wind-resistant food crops such as sweet corn (used as an effective windbreak in market gardens in Holland), sunflowers, cardoons, chicory, and Jerusalem artichokes. This type of windscreen is even used in commercial vegetable gardens.

The range of boundary materials available to the kitchen gardener is so large and varied that choosing the right materials, dimensions, and style for any one situation becomes an exciting adventure.

Arbors, Arches, and Tunnels

Because of the nature of their plantings, kitchen gardens tend to be horizontal and low in scale. To achieve a satisfying overall design, it is necessary to provide some vertical elements to counteract the prevailing horizontal impression. Arbors, arches, tunnels, and pergolas are the usual devices used for this purpose. When well designed and judiciously located, they also provide the garden with one or a series of focal points—features on which the eye can rest a moment during a visual exploration of the garden.

Two approaches can be taken to the design of these vertical elements: they can be conceived as architectural constructs, fully decorative in their own right, or they can be thought of as behind-the-scene structures destined to be lost under an abundance of climbing plants. Regardless of

Garden tunnels have been constructed with hazel rods since the medieval period. Here, they support French beans and arch over the new tunnels constructed in the kitchen garden of His Royal Highness, the Prince of Wales, at Highgrove, Gloucestershire, England.

an orchard with many "goodly allies with roosting places covered thoroughly with white thorn and hazell." For "allies" read "alleys" or "walks," and for "roosting places" read "resting places" or "arbors." In the seventeenth century, features like these were usually built out of elaborate trelliswork using Spanish chestnut wood. By the end of the eighteenth and the beginning of the nineteenth century, the use of iron resulted in tunnels and arbors so light and elegant in design that the climbing plants that grew on them tended to have a stronger visual impact than the structures themselves. This design tendency was prominent in the late nineteenth century, when such structures were made out of a combination of iron and thin galvanized wire.

ARBORS

John Worlidge, the most practical of the late seventeenth-century English gardening writers, advised that, "For cool recesses in the hottest times, it has

the approach, these structures have been used in gardens for centuries. They have been depicted on wall paintings unearthed from the buried city of Pompeii, in medieval illuminated manuscripts, and in early gardening books.

We know that in the sixteenth century they were often formed with flexible hazel or willow rods. A 1521 inventory of Thornbury Castle in England lists

been useful to erect or frame arbors with poles or rods." They are particularly useful in a kitchen garden where working or cropping can be arduous under the summer sun. There is often a pressing need for a few minutes' rest in an arbor's shade. The coolest shade is provided by a leafy arbor of entwined branches. The flexible branches of willow, hazel, or quince are ideal for forming living arbors, although they may need an initial, temporary support of bamboo canes or iron rods that can be discarded once the shape of the arbor is formed. However, arbors made of trellis make an immediate impact and are not too costly or time-consuming to construct. In a damp climate, however, it may be short-lived because its many wooden joints can rot.

Careful, annual scrutiny is required to identify and repair rotting sections. For this to be practical, the climbers growing on the arbor should be annuals, or, if they are perennials, they should be able to survive very hard pruning so that they can be cut to ground level each year to allow careful examination of the trelliswork. Ironwork arbors are more durable but not as simple to erect as trelliswork, which can be assembled by a carpenter on site. Ironwork has to be carefully planned in advance and then manufactured in a workshop. It needs occasional repainting,

At St. Mary's Farm, Berkshire, England, metal arches support cordon apples and pears and frame the view into the garden.

so climbers must be chosen that tolerate temporary removal. A reliable technique is to grow climbers on removable lattice or wire mesh panels fixed between the iron supports. These panels, together with their climbers, can then be eased away from the main structure to allow repainting.

Suitable climbing plants for arbors are:

1. **Climbing fruit**
   a. *Vitis vinifera* 'Purpurea': Its purple foliage is very effective with silver-leaved plants.
   b. *Vitis* 'Brant': This hybrid vine produces numerous bunches of sweet, aromatic grapes.
   c. *Vitis vinifera* 'Apiifolia': It is called the "parsley vine" because of its deeply cut foliage.
   d. *Rubus laciniatus* 'Oregon Thornless': This cut-leaved blackberry produces ten-foot-long canes each year.

2. **Climbing vegetables**
   Runner beans: Some vigorous varieties reaching twelve feet each year are suitable. Their delicate scarlet flowers are followed by hanging beans that can be cropped as you sit.

3. **Climbing flowers**
   a. Sweet peas: Their scent will make the arbor even more pleasant to sit in.
   b. *Cobaea scandens* 'Cathedral Bells': This easy-to-grow Mexican climber has substantial, bell-like flowers.
   c. *Asarina scandens:* Snapdragonlike flowers bloom until Christmas if no frosts prevail.
   d. *Tropaeolum canariense:* This climbing nasturtium has canary yellow flowers and pale green foliage.

ARCHES

Arches are the ideal vertical element to use in a small garden, because they give height while occupying a minimum of ground space. If used as a support for runner beans or cordon fruit, precious ground space is further maximized. Aesthetically, arches can be used to frame a view into or out of the garden; they have even been used to form a productive porch or entry to a country cottage. If combined in series, arches can form a tunnel.

TUNNELS

Small-bed kitchen gardens depend on extensive path networks. Some of the space needed for these paths can be brought into use by covering them with tunnels of climbing fruit or vegetables. In selecting a path to cover, give preference to one running east and west, so that the plants on both sides of the structure get equal amounts of sun. Tunnel frameworks can be made of wood, iron, or the expensive but long-lasting and maintenance-free plastic-coated metal. A pleasant effect is achieved by shaping the top of the tunnel as a half circle or a half ellipse. Estimating dimensions can be a tricky task. The tunnel at Barnsley, on which gourds, runner beans, sweet peas, roses, and nasturtiums grow, is, for example, 7 feet high and 6½ feet wide. Its uprights are spaced 30 inches along its length and its horizontal wires are placed at 2-foot vertical intervals. At Hillbarn, the tunnel of hazelnuts is 11 feet high and 11 feet wide, with nut trees planted at 5-foot centers. Also at Hillbarn, the pear tunnel is 10 feet high and 8 feet wide, and the arches are at 10-foot intervals.

(continued on p. 77)

Hillbarn House, Wiltshire, England

MR. AND MRS. ALASTAIR BUCHANAN

Quince arches, a pear arcade, and a nut tunnel all provide a living architectural framework to the kitchen garden at Hillbarn. They also give the essential element of height to its design. Planned by American garden designer Lanning Roper over 25 years ago, they have been maintained ever since by the head gardener, John Last.

The quince arches are made from the variety 'Portugal', which has the most flexible wood. No supporting ironwork was used. One tree, with a clear 3-foot high stem, was planted on each side of the

The silvery foliage of the quince arch acts as a background for the standard roses in the herb beds.

The nut tunnel was formed by training selected stems of hazelnut over a skeletal structure of bamboo canes.

pathway. Three or four of its leaders were selected to grow from its main stem and the others were discarded. Using short lengths of bamboo cane for temporary support as the leaders grew, they were gradually trained over the path to form an archway. The lateral growths, which are often flimsy, can be plaited to strengthen the living structure. Annual maintenance consists of simply shortening the lateral growths to about 4 inches. The arches are now twenty-five years old and have reached 9 feet in height and width. They are at their most beautiful in April, with abundant pink flowers and silvery leaves.

The pear arcades that surround the garden are twenty-five years old. The arches, at 10-foot intervals along the paths, are each composed of a pair of arches in angle iron set 2 feet apart and braced by rods every 1 foot in height. Surprisingly, the arch bases are not set in concrete because, as John Last explains, although the arches support the pears initially, it is the pears that support the arches eventually, as a result of the strong hold their root systems take on the soil. Each leader is trained flat against the arch's upright and the laterals grow out toward the light. The effect of these spurs when they flower in April and May is as entrancing as when they are hung with fruit in late summer. Three important points should be kept in mind while training:

a. When young, pears should be winter-pruned. After six years, they should be summer-pruned, with each of the laterals shortened to three or four buds only.
b. Separate the young stems from the ironwork with rubber pads or bands. Otherwise, chafing of the stems will result, especially during windy conditions.
c. As constant pruning weakens the trees, it is essential to top-dress them with a couple of ounces of sulfate of potash each February and a mulch of farmyard manure in most years.

The most interesting of the garden's living architectural features is the nut tunnel. Cobnuts and filberts—both hazel trees selected for the size and flavor of their nuts—were planted at 5-foot centers, in a line on each side of one of the garden paths. Hazels form multi-stemmed trunks by nature. Every year, three or four of the straightest stems were selected from the clump, and the others were removed. When these stems reached 10 feet in height, they were linked across the top with a line of bamboo canes. Then the flexible lateral shoots were bent over the pathway, using more bamboo canes to tie them overhead. Gradually, a ribcage of bamboo was established to support all the new growth.

Important points to remember in maintaining the tunnel are:

a. Use tarred string rather than wire for tying. It will last only a few seasons, but wire will cut into the hazels' soft new growth. Nicking the surface of the cane with a knife will hold the string in place even during high winds.

b. As stems get older they produce fewer leaves. They should be taken out and replaced with younger stems that were allowed to grow for this purpose.

c. Thin the trees each year by shortening all the lateral shoots to about 4 inches. This is best done in January, because buds may have already started to break by February.

d. Although it is difficult, it is worthwhile when pruning to keep as much of the catkin wood as possible. The effect of the pendulous catkins in the tunnel during spring is ravishing.

It is the expert maintenance of these fruit features that gives to Hillbarn a character unlike any other garden featured here.

Left: Whimsical topiaries, like this swan, provide light, decorative relief among the ordered rows of vegetables and fruits.

Below: Gourds, runner beans, sweet peas, roses, and nasturtiums grow over the tunnel at Barnsley House, England.

Tunnel Types

1. Tree fruit tunnels: In early spring, their pink or white blossoms transform the drab, post-winter landscape. In late summer and autumn, fruit is the reward. Select only free-growing varieties with fresh-looking foliage.

a. Apple tunnel: This is an ideal feature for the colder garden, as it generally does not blossom until early May. Place posts and their arches 12 to 15 feet apart. Stretch 14-gauge galvanized wires *between* the posts at 15- to 18-inch vertical intervals; plant the trees halfway between a pair of posts and gradually espalier them into the tunnel shape.

b. Pear tunnel: This is the best choice for warmer gardens, as it flowers earlier, usually in April. The posts and their arches should be placed a little closer than for apples, between 10 and 12 feet apart, and the wiring at 10- to 12-inch vertical intervals.

c. Nut tunnel: Tunnels can also be made of cobnut and filberts, species of *Corylus* selected for the reliability and size of their nuts. The purple filbert, *C. maxima* 'Purpurea', is dramatic, with its purple spring foliage and wine-red catkins. Twelve feet between the trees, 8 to 10 feet for the height of the tunnel, and 12- to 15-inch vertical intervals between the espalier wires are the recommended dimensions.

d. Fig tunnel: In a mild climate, figs can be used to make a productive tunnel, although the

birds may get the fruit if it is not protected by nets while ripening. Trees should be planted 12 to 15 feet apart and 14-gauge wire or 4-ply string should be stretched between the posts at 1-foot vertical intervals.

e. Citrus tunnel: Citrus fruits are a traditional feature of Mediterranean gardens, where they enjoy warm summers and mild winters. There are famous old examples constructed with a painted timber framework at the Villa Carlotta on Lake Como in Italy.

2. Soft fruit tunnels:

a. Vine tunnel: This is a notable feature of Mediterranean gardens, where, constructed of a light metal framework, they often shade the garden's principal walks. They are also encountered in *trompe l'oeil* paintings on the walls and ceilings of the internal corridors and loggias of Renaissance and baroque palaces throughout Europe. Thus, the mem-

ory of warm, sunlit days was conjured up in the midst of the bleakest winter months. To make a real vine tunnel, plant vines 4 to 5 feet apart and grow them on arches 8 to 10 feet apart between a pair of 14-gauge galvanized wires stretched to zigzag at 1-foot vertical intervals. A spectacular modern example is at the home of a famous Chianti wine, the Abbadia a Coltibuono, south of Florence.

In Tasha Tudor's garden near Brattleboro, Vermont, the bean tunnels are constructed of bamboo canes and string. They can be relocated in the garden each year to ensure good crop rotation.

(continued on p. 85)

Highgrove, Gloucestershire, England

H.R.H., THE PRINCE OF WALES

Tunnels of fruit and vegetables form the principal features of the newly re-created kitchen garden at Highgrove. The most prominent is an apple tunnel constructed of iron hoops; the apple trees span high and wide over the central path

Tunnels of fruit and vegetables form the principal organizing features of the redesigned kitchen garden.

Opposite: A doorway frames the garden's cross-path. It leads to a latticework arbor—a gift from The Worshipful Company of Fruiterers.

Right: Dennis Brown, who is in charge of the kitchen garden.

that divides the garden in two. Such tunnels were a feature of nineteenth-century kitchen gardens. Here, they are at their most spectacular in spring, when they are in flower and the lacelike tracery of their trained branches casts intricately patterned shadows across the path underneath. Unfortunately, fruit trees eventually become bare at the base. At Highgrove, a row of dwarf apples has been espaliered on a wire fence below the standard apples. These are supplemented by low hedges of the spice-scented sweet

Left: A smaller number of lettuces bolt to form decorative cones of foliage, breaking an otherwise over-regimented pattern.

Right: As part of the conservation of old fruit varieties—a work which is a specialty of the garden—pears are espaliered to perfection on the garden's walls.

Left: Meticulous cultivation ensures luxuriant pear crops.

Opposite: Carrots are grown in many varieties, providing black, purple, yellow, white, and red roots, as well as the traditional orange.

grass paths lead to secluded, shady arbors of the same construction. In each have been placed fuchsia-filled Italian terra-cotta jars as focal points, and wooden benches for quiet reflection. The atmosphere inside these arbors is like that of a miniature forest glade.

Sizable quantities of vegetables are grown in these beds, which feed a number of households on this large estate. Dennis Brown, the head gardener, grows the vegetables in traditional rows, as opposed to the small blocks of the contemporary *potager*. Innumerable heads of admirably grown brassicas— cabbages, cauliflowers, and brussels sprouts—in one bed are matched by a similar phalanx of lettuces, with different forms and colors, in another. As at Barnsley House, some of the lettuces are deliberately left in the ground: as they mature, they form decorative cones of foliage that help to break the formality of the regularly planted beds. Carrots are grown in over ten different varieties, including some that produce roots of unusual colors: black, purple, yellow, white, and red. Many of these varieties originated in the eighteenth century and are seldom grown now because of their low yields and weak disease resistance. However, the Prince of Wales believes it is important to preserve them, as they may be valuable as breeding stock in the future. His concern for this kind of conservation is further illustrated by his recent rescue of the financially troubled Brogdale Experimental Horticultural Station in Kent, where rare fruit varieties have been maintained for many years.

In the re-creation of the kitchen garden at Highgrove, the Prince of Wales was helped by Lady Salisbury, whose own garden at Hatfield contains a wealth of interesting planting and design ideas.

briar roses. Together, the foliage of the dwarf apples and the sweet briar roses make up for any loss of foliage at the base of the apple arches. Thick clumps of hellebores and primroses have been planted at the fruit trees' feet to give flower color in late winter and early spring.

A path bordered by scented roses (which increase the pleasure of summer gardening) crosses the apple tunnel and divides the garden into four quarters. Each quarter is subdivided by smaller tunnels of French beans and sweet peas supported on delicate hoops of flexible hazel rods. Underneath, quiet

b. Blackberry tunnel: The 'Oregon Thornless' variety with its 10-foot-long canes and its parsley-shaped leaves that look good even in winter is the ideal subject for this kind of tunnel. The uprights and arches should be set in the ground 3 to 4 feet apart; the horizontal wires stretching between them should be at 1-foot vertical intervals.

3. Vegetable tunnels: No other climbing vegetable exceeds the 10 or 12 feet achieved by the most vigorous varieties of runner bean. In fact, most climbing vegetables have a maximum height of 6 to 8 feet. They are therefore only suitable for covering the narrowest paths.

a. Runner bean tunnel: The uprights and arches should be just 1 foot apart and the horizontal wires should be placed at 6-inch intervals. Superb examples can be seen at Highgrove, where the tunnels are formed of bent hazel rods.

b. Squash tunnel: Although normally grown along the ground, summer squashes can be grown as climbers up to 7 or 8 feet, just sufficient to cover a narrow tunnel. The uprights, arches, and wires should be at the same distances as the runner bean tunnel. There are many new small and shapely varieties now available, including a new variety known as vegetable spaghetti, as well as many decorative varieties of brightly colored and interestingly marked gourds. A medley of edible and decorative varieties would make an amusing scheme.

c. French bean tunnel: As French beans rarely reach more than 6 or 7 feet in height, they need to be supplemented with taller-growing runner beans if a full tunnel is to be formed. Four-inch-square galvanized mesh, rather than horizontal wires, should be stretched between the uprights.

d. Cucumber tunnel: Usually thought of as a greenhouse crop outside the United States, there are many new outdoor varieties with improved flavor, including Japanese climbing varieties with large decorative leaves that will grow to a height of 6 feet.

PERGOLAS

In hot climates, the construction of a pergola is the best way to provide shade for walkways. In cooler climates, its usefulness is in displaying climbing flowers and fruit. It may be conceived as a focal point of the garden's overall design or as a discreet feature set to one side and entirely smothered in plants. In either case, a simple wooden or iron structure is more becoming for a kitchen garden than an elaborate one of brick or stone, such as one sees in purely decorative gardens. The bare wood may seem stark at first, but the growing plants will soon soften it. The frame should be sturdy enough to bear the weight of mature climbing plants, and stronger still in areas that may receive heavy snowfall. As with a tunnel, an east–west orientation is preferable, so that plants on both sides of the pergola get equal amounts of sun. A location along the northern boundary of the garden helps to minimize shade to low-growing vegetables. The architectural style should match that of the house. A formal, period house should have a pergola with a strong architectural design, whereas a country cottage would benefit from one of a simpler, rustic design. A pergola walk leads the eye along its length and demands some suitable ornament, plant, or view as a terminal focus. Pergola posts should be centered at not less than 10 feet and have a minimum height of 7 feet.

Pergola Types

1. Grapevine pergola: Hardy vines provide the most attractive overhead shade, with variable leaf color that is particularly rich in autumn. Hanging bunches of grapes are also easy to thin and harvest from underneath. Climbing by means of tendrils, the vines twine along a network of wires between the main supports.

2. Passion fruit pergola: Another twiner that will appreciate wires between the main supports, the passion fruit, *Passiflora edulis*, has beautiful flowers, succeeded after hot summers by egg-shaped yellow fruit.

3. Kiwi pergola: The kiwi, or Chinese gooseberry, *Actinidia chinensis*, is a very vigorous, deciduous twiner that is hardy to Zone 8. Its large, heart-shaped leaves are born on reddish, hairy shoots. There is a splendid example laid out on a curve in the Val Rahmeh garden near Menton in the South of France.

FRUIT CAGES

One of the problems with growing berry fruit is that birds—particularly blackbirds, finches, sparrows, starlings, tits, and thrushes—are hell-bent on eating it. From the moment the berries turn color, they have to be protected by fine-mesh plastic or metal netting. This can be thrown over the bushes for the requisite few weeks of the year and, if black or dark green, it is not too unsightly to use for such a short period. Birds will get the small amount of fruit that protrudes through the netting, but this is usually acceptable as long as the major portion of the crop is saved.

To preserve the entire crop, the erection of a fruit cage is necessary. Lightweight plastic cages are now sold in modules so that you can assemble one of a suitable size and shape. They can be sited temporarily when required and then disassembled and moved into storage for the rest of the year. They are even light enough to be moved easily around the garden to protect a succession of fruit in different locations. Fruit cages can also be sited permanently. Year-round fruit cages offer the added advantage of protecting the fruit buds—also a favorite of birds—during the winter. (The over-wintering buds of cherries, greengages, purple plums, and most bush fruits are particularly popular.) A cage might be constructed of posts at least 7 feet high, set approximately 6 feet apart. Wires stretched from post to post can support $\frac{1}{2}$- to $\frac{3}{4}$-inch wire, polyethylene, or nylon netting. However, wire netting should not be used for the top of the cage as zinc toxicity may result when condensation drops from its galvanized coating. The netting should be left on throughout the year except during heavy snowfall, and it should be opened during flowering time to allow freer access to pollinating insects.

When a fruit cage is to be permanent, considerable thought should be given to its decorative design. In the National Trust garden of West Green House in Hampshire, England, the famous octagonal fruit cage, which looks like a giant, baroque aviary, is a good example of ornamental design. More restrained and rational are the equally decorative fruit cages at Cromwell's Fort in Ireland. As there has been no tradition in Western gardening of ornamental fruit cages, it is difficult to find models on which to base a design. Aviary designs are good substitutes, because their scale and function are very similar to those of a fruit cage.

Greenhouses, Potting Sheds, and Garden Houses

An arbor gives shade from the sun but not shelter from cold and rain. A garden house, a greenhouse, or a potting shed is required for this—particularly if the kitchen garden is located a long way from the house. To have all three would be an excessive luxury in all but the largest kitchen gardens. In a small garden, it is advisable to design a multipurpose structure. There are few precedents in garden design for such a combination, but a starting point can be found in the traditional orangery that served as garden house, greenhouse, and occasionally as a potting shed.

Any structure of this kind would dominate a small garden with its sheer bulk. Careful consideration should be given to location and design. There are two approaches: either

Above: A combination garden house and toolshed in John Saladino's kitchen garden in Connecticut.

Left: The "Gothick" garden house in the kitchen garden of Glin Castle, Ireland, is deliberately escapist in style.

Frost-tender vegetables may be started inside a greenhouse like this one in the kitchen garden of the Chateau de St. Jean-de-Beauregard, France. Here, warm soil encourages early seed germination.

design a dramatic structure that will act as a focus for the whole garden, or develop a discreet design that will be primarily functional and can be tucked away in one corner behind an espaliered apple or other screen. A dramatic building should be either at the center of the garden or at the end of one of the main vistas, perhaps where it can easily be seen from the house. In fact, a position near the house will make it easier to install services such as electricity and water. If the structure is actually attached to the house, the gardener will have direct access to it without having to brave winter rain or cold.

Over-detailed structures are not appropriate for a kitchen garden, because one of its purposes is to act as a foil and support for plants. Simple but elegantly proportioned buildings should be designed in materials appropriate to their setting. Pinewood looks good in conifer country, limestone in limestone country, brick if the house and garden walls are already in brick. The bulk of the building can be minimized by designing it en suite with a second architectural structure, such as a pergola, or by surrounding with it boldly scaled plants, such as globe artichokes.

GREENHOUSES

There are two reasons to build a greenhouse in a kitchen garden. The first is to start tender vegetables early and to be able to extend the cropping season of hardy ones. In temperate climates, short, cool summers prevent tender vegetables, such as tomatoes, peppers, eggplants, cucumbers, and okra, from reaching full maturity before they are killed by frost in the late summer or fall. Therefore, they must be started inside, where the warm greenhouse soil will encourage early seed germination. The plants can then either mature inside the house or be planted out in the garden after the danger of spring frost has passed. In this way, also, crops of French and runner beans, peas, onions, leeks, sweet corn, cabbages, and cauliflower can be ready for eating weeks earlier than normal.

The greenhouse in the old kitchen garden of the Chateau de Miromesnil, Normandy, France, is efficiently located.

The second reason for a greenhouse is to grow tender fruit and to extend the cropping season of some of the hardy fruits. Although grapes, melons, peaches, nectarines, and figs will fruit outside in favorable locations in a temperate climate, they will fruit with more reliability and abundance in a greenhouse. Also, very tender fruit—oranges, lemons, and olives—can be grown in a greenhouse in pots and tubs and then set out to decorate the garden paths in summer. In addition, early-maturing crops of hardy fruit can be enjoyed from the greenhouse. For example, strawberries grown in the garden will be ready for eating in June or July, but those grown in a cold greenhouse will be ready in May. Grown in a heated greenhouse, strawberries will be delicious to eat as early as March.

Location and Construction

From a functional aspect, the ideal greenhouse is designed as a lean-to and set against a sheltered, south-facing wall to reduce cold winds and maximize heat from the low winter sun. Even if there is no south-facing wall available, an east–west orientation is best. A minimum size of 10 feet by 8 feet is essential to give enough wall and roof space to grow peaches, nectarines, vines, or figs. The form of construction depends on the site. In an exposed location, walls that are solid for the bottom 2 to 3 feet will lose less heat than walls that are entirely glass. In a sheltered loca-

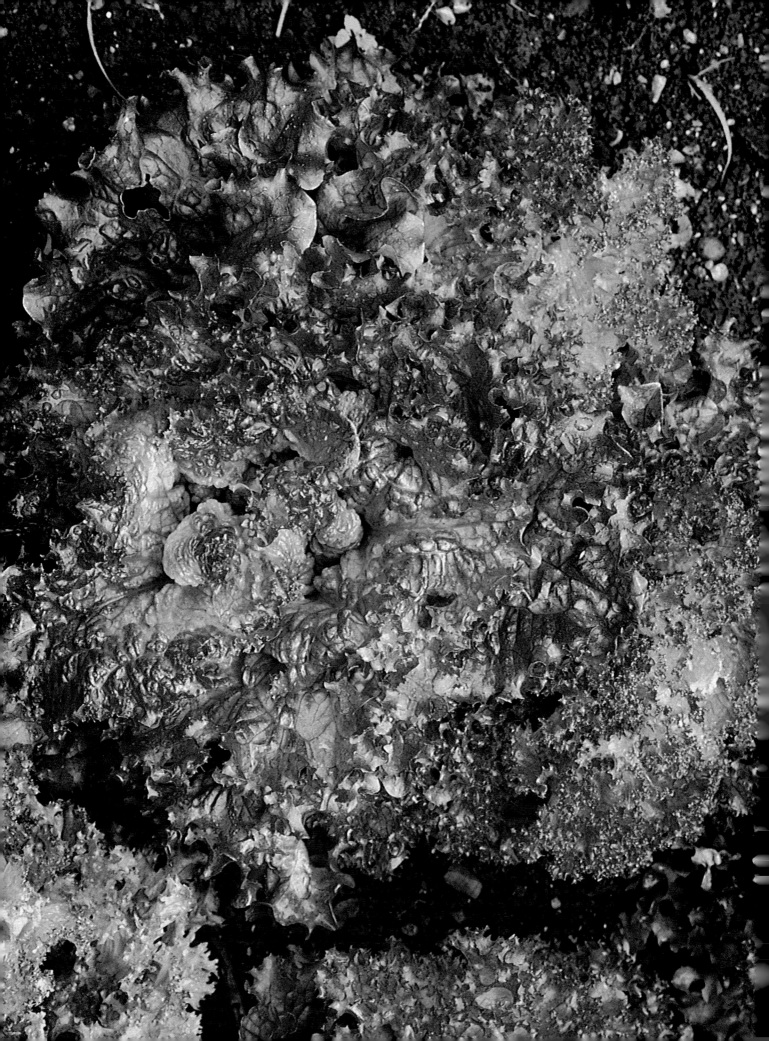

tion, glass walls extending to the ground and angled to the sun will maximize light and warmth to the interior. Although a greenhouse attached to the house is ideal because it can be reached without going outside in winter, its prominent position may require a decorative and expensive design. The small greenhouse in the National Trust garden of Peckover in England shows how, with cast-iron or other enrichments, including colorful floor tile patterns and slatted shelving painted brilliant white, an ornamental effect can be achieved.

On the other hand, light, prefabricated greenhouses in aluminum or wood can look jarring or too dominant in a small garden. They are better screened from view, behind, for example, an espaliered apple fence that will also shade the house from excessive summer heat and allow maximum light through its bare branches in winter. Regarding the internal fittings of the greenhouse and their operation, technology has come to the aid of the gardener. No longer is there the worry of temperamental stoves, the endless opening and closing of windows, and the tedious business of watering by hand. Ventilation, fumigation, humidity, and heat inside the house can now be automatically controlled, as can summer shading by means of slatted summer blinds.

Cases and Frames

Those without space for a full-sized greenhouse can opt for what is known as a glazed—or conservatory—case running along the length of one of the garden walls. Unfortunately, as there are none available commercially, they must be custom made. Such a case consists of narrow, glazed units erected against

Opposite: The dull tones of this lettuce help bring contrasting colors together and allow for easier visual transitions in the garden.

a wall to protect tender wall fruit, and accessible from the front by means of hinged or removable glazed casements. The most famous example is in the garden of Chatsworth in England, although it is on a scale hardly viable today.

Those without space or money to erect a greenhouse or case may have to relinquish the idea of growing tender fruit, but they can still grow tender vegetables with a low glazed frame. These can be bought prefabricated and with all the automatically controlled equipment available for full-scale greenhouses—ventilators, heaters, and irrigators.

THE POTTING SHED

A service area is as important to a garden as a kitchen is to a house. Just as many people no longer want a kitchen that is merely functional, neither do they want an inadequate work area in the garden. Too often in the past, the work area was not planned in advance but added to piecemeal, until it evolved into a kind of garden slum. Today, the work area benefits from good compact design and the intelligent use of modern materials. Concrete floors inside and out are easy to hose down, plastic shelves and potting benches are a cinch to install, and the aluminum structure of a greenhouse or frame saves puttying and painting.

A good functional design will provide space for:

1. tools;
2. pots, seed pans, and trays;
3. soil and compost; and
4. a mini-office area.

A little office, with desk, bulletin board, drawers and shelves for notes and records, files, seed catalogs, planting plans, seed packets, and books, is most helpful for on-site organization. The minimum size of a full-scale potting shed, like that of a full-scale greenhouse, is about 8 by 10 feet. Where space is at a premium, an outdoor potting cupboard, or, in a mild climate such as found in California, a simple lath-shaded work area, can be used instead.

GARDEN HOUSES

The most elaborate and costly garden house ever built for a kitchen garden might well be the Pavilion of Aurora at Sceaux near Paris. Presiding over a *potager* designed by Le Notre for Louis XIV's great minister, Colbert, it is an enormous, stone-faced rotunda with an interior designed by the court painter, Charles le Brun. Another garden house, more modest but nonetheless famous, is in Thomas Jefferson's vegetable garden at Monticello. It is brick, just 12 feet 6 inches square, and its pyramidal roof is hidden behind a Chinese-style balustrade. The domed octagon erected by George Washington

in the Upper Garden at Mount Vernon is another example of a garden house designed to bold effect.

Although the Mount Vernon garden house was recently copied by the couturier Hubert Givenchy for his *potager* in Normandy, France, most modern kitchen gardens require a simpler, more modest structure. In addition to being picturesque, a garden house should offer pleasant seating. In fact, a truly successful garden house should accommodate a range of needs, including shade from summer sun (but enough light to read by) and shelter from the wind (especially important for *al fresco* meals), and it should still provide a pleasant view of the garden. In some locations, discretion should be thrown to the wind and the garden house elevated from the ordinary with a deliberately escapist style—perhaps *chinoiserie*, Islamic, or gothic.

Opposite: The eye is attracted by glass bell cloches (in use to protect young seedlings) among newly planted broccoli. A low "apple fence" closes the view behind.

Seats and Other Garden Ornaments

Every book on garden ornament recommends that objects should be appropriate for their setting. In the kitchen garden, therefore, this suggests that ornamentation should be a combination of beauty and utility. Useful ornaments, such as an antique beehive, an old lead cistern, or a row of decorative pots, seem more appropriate than elaborate representational sculpture overloaded with gratuitous meaning and decoration. However, if figurative sculpture is to be used in the kitchen garden, it should be chosen to support, rather than distract from, the garden's theme. A figure of Ceres (the goddess of the harvest) or Pomona (the goddess of fruit), a cornucopia of vegetables, or a simple pineapple—all traditional forms of carved stone sculpture—could enhance a kitchen garden's theme.

Regardless of the subject, garden sculpture can suffer from over-refinement. A highly worked, finely carved piece in rich materials will rarely fit in a kitchen garden. However, if modest and well proportioned, a sculpture will be suitably discreet among the vegetable patterns. A garden can also be spoiled by over-crowding with ornament: an elaborate assortment of decoration overlying a rich planting scheme can add up to an indigestible whole.

Ornament can be used strongly, for example at the center of the garden to draw the entire design together, or more modestly, as a focus in one part of the garden only. Sited at the end of a vista, ornament will draw attention to itself, but used in pairs along the length of a vista, it can be used to lead the eye to something else, like a view or a summer house.

Top: An unusual combination of timber and wicker characterize this seat in the kitchen garden in Lakeville, Connecticut.

Above: A country baroque seat in the walled garden at Leixlip Castle, Ireland.

Left: A café chair in Mrs. Bunny Williams's Connecticut garden.

Right: A café table and chairs (painted in a two-color scheme) in Ryan Gainey's kitchen garden in Atlanta, Georgia.

Below: An antique wicker trolley and ornamental staking grace the Williams's kitchen garden in Connecticut.

The ornament's material should also be appropriate to the setting. A granite trough or bowl will look harmonious in granite country, but not in a garden where brick is the primary building material. There are occasional circumstances in which an ornament can be successfully used deliberately to contrast with its surroundings, but, more often, by drawing attention to itself, it will distract from the impact of the rest of the garden.

ANTIQUE GARDENING TOOLS AND EQUIPMENT

Whereas antique statues and urns may look pretentious in a kitchen garden, ornament that is founded on function does not. A seat can be a straightforward functional feature, but it can also be conceived as an elaborate sculptured object while still retaining its original purpose. Antique or finely crafted sundials, drinking fountains, or rainwater butts are appropriate ornaments. The dipping cisterns in the Upper Garden at Mount Vernon in Virginia and at Stavordale Priory in Somerset, England, seem just right in their kitchen garden settings. The deliberately casual arrangements of antique garden pots, watering cans, and baskets along the path of Nancy McCabe's garden in Connecticut seem similarly fitting.

(continued on p. 107)

Falls Village, Connecticut, United States

MRS. NANCY MCCABE

The masterly use of antique building materials and garden ornament is the key attraction of Nancy McCabe's kitchen garden. They impart a convincingly aged look to what is really a young garden. Interestingly, none of her antique ornaments are restored. They are "conserved"—the aging process is arrested yet the antique patina with all its imperfections remains. Further, Nancy McCabe has mastered the art of making her garden look, as some interior decorators have learned to do with rooms, as if the owner has left just for a moment and is about to return. A half-filled trug of cut herbs, a wicker basket of just-pulled weeds, or a pair of antique secateurs is often found lying decorously along one of the paths, giving the garden that indefinable, lived-in look.

The garden, which is only 24 by 33 feet in size, has an immediately informal atmosphere result-ing from its four boundaries that are not uniform either in their design or in their planting. One side is occupied by the wall of the house. A second is formed by a high yew hedge. A third is formed with a high trellis fence and archway, all painted a dark "dale green." (The archway is crowned with gun-metal squirrels once used as targets in a shooting gallery!) The last side is bounded by an espaliered apple fence, with apples being trained on television aerial guy wires held down by some of Mr. McCabe's collection of antique weights.

The garden is divided into four quarters by paths of antique bricks

The garden entrance is through a latticework archway crowned with a pair of gunmetal squirrels that were originally used as targets in a shooting gallery.

Left: A cast-iron water pump, terra-cotta edgings from Savannah, Georgia, and from Charleston, South Carolina, and a wicker weed basket are just some of the antique ornaments that adorn this garden.

Left: The delicate *Lotus berthelotii* trails over an antique terra-cotta jar.

Below: The paths are constructed using antique bricks rescued from a demolition in Winstead, Connecticut. The wicker chair is a nineteenth-century piece from the Adirondacks.

rescued from the demolition of a nineteenth-century building in Winstead, Connecticut. The brickwork is worth careful study. First, it was laid in many different patterns—basketweave, herringbone, chevron—so one is kept constantly alert while walking around. Second, the width of the joints between the bricks is deliberately varied from a quarter inch to an inch to give a natural look. Further, the joints are recessed below the level of the paving, so the mosses and seedlings that gather there soften the

Rhubarb and kale are blanched in jars from the Wichford Pottery, Warwickshire, and from Clifton Nurseries, London, England.

hard outlines of the bricks. Third, the brick pattern is varied by the occasional insertion of pieces of stone, usually *objets trouvés,* such as the white marble threshold stone from a house in Waterbury, Connecticut, and by path edgings of antique terra-cotta manufactured in Charleston and Savannah for decorative use along sidewalks and in cemeteries. Finally, the overall rectangular plan has been broken by the deliberate laying of just one path at an odd angle. This is a device frequently used by Nancy McCabe to introduce the unexpected, thus preventing the design from becoming too predictable and boring.

Exploring the rich and complex patterns of these pathways, one keeps discovering another garden object from Nancy McCabe's collection. Many have a semi-industrial origin and are both practical and decorative, making them so appropriate in a kitchen garden setting. An old copper container turns out to have been, in its original existence, part of a 1911 patent electric washing machine manufactured in Syracuse, New York. The antique watering can bears the stamp of Maurice Crimonceaux with an address in Paris at the Quai de la Megisseraie, the traditional home of all good French seedsmen and garden suppliers. A wicker chair, painted black-green, turns out to be a nineteenth-century piece from the Adirondacks. A Dutch ceramic dog bowl and a nineteenth-century footscraper by the kitchen door complete the main vista. However, not all of the ornaments are antique. No less interesting are the elegant brass plant supports, row markers, and plant labels that are manufactured locally to McCabe's own design.

The beds, no more than 6 feet wide for easy access, contain alkaline soil kept 3 inches above the surrounding path level to improve drainage. Dwarf lavender, in both the 'Hidcote' and the 'Munstead' varieties, line the principal paths fronting a collection of vegetables and herbs chosen for their elegant texture and discreet color tones. Lines of fine-leaved herbs like sage, dill, mint, and thyme divide contrasting lines of curly leaved kale, crinkly leaved Savoy cabbage, feathery-foliaged fennel, and cut-leaved lettuce in plantings that demonstrate the remarkable range of vegetable textures. Flower color is provided by allowing the occasional foxglove to seed among the salad onions, and also by setting out

pots of tender plants from the greenhouse during the summer. Passionflowers climbing on bamboo canes appear prominently, as do tall statuesque plants, often with currently fashionable tubular flowerheads, such as acidantheras, nicotianas, hostas, and galtonias. From behind one of them peeps a pretty pottery hedgehog.

Recently, Nancy McCabe has created a second kitchen garden in quite a different location in her

The remarkable range of texture and color tone in vegetable foliage is displayed in this lavender-edged bed.

garden. It is a complete contrast in both style and planting to the first. Its keynote is its locust-wood furniture and fencing presented in a totally original style that unexpectedly blends traditional Adirondack and exotic *chinoiserie* styles. The planting is strikingly unlike that of the first garden, in which pale and subtle colors only are used. Here, the emphasis is on brightly colored vegetables and fruits from South America, including yellow and currant-sized tomato varieties as well as many standard ones, sweet peppers of yellow, red, and green varieties, and peas and beans with various flower and pod colors. A rich variety of honeysuckles, morning glories, and roses—including the rose called, because of the curious shape of its flowers, *Rosa* 'Chapeau de Napoleon'—clamber along the enclosing fence.

The cosmopolitan sources of the seed and ornament in the garden give it an intriguing sophistication. The radish and chicory are grown from seed packets purchased along Paris's Quai de la Megisseraie, the rhubarb is blanched in forcing jars from the Wichford Pottery and Clifton Nurseries, both in England. Yet home sources are not neglected. Nancy McCabe trawls the seed lists issued from Jefferson's garden at Monticello and from commercial firms like Shepherd's, Stokes', and The Cook's Garden for suitable varieties.

Garden ornament that is fanciful but functional and garden furniture that is imaginative in design yet comfortable are the focal points of Nancy McCabe's kitchen gardens.

PLANT CONTAINERS

The ubiquitous plant container, including a wide range of pots, tubs, troughs, barrels, and baskets, is a garden ornament that is both decorative and functional. Like all outdoor ornaments, they should be sturdy, bold, and weather resistant. They are sometimes so large that their weight makes it difficult to

move them, so they become permanent or semipermanent fixtures. In pairs, they mark the entrance to a pathway. In lines, they give rhythm to a vista. On a plinth, they can be used to give height to the design. By corners, steps, or along a terrace wall, they act as punctuation. Luxuriantly planted, they soften large paved areas where plants could not otherwise grow, and they are ideal for showing off delicately detailed plants that would be lost in the midst of a larger planting.

This movable bean tent was photographed soon after the beans were planted out.

A length of cheesecloth serving as a cloche to protect young lettuces illustrates Nancy McCabe's inventive approach to garden design in Falls Village, Connecticut.

Some containers are small enough to be moved around, not only from year to year, but also from season to season to vary the accents of color. Pots of annual flowers act as ideal markers in any design and should be treated as if they were flower arrangements. The pots should be turned frequently to expose all of the plants to equal amounts of sunlight, and the plants should be replaced regularly so the arrangements always look their best. Such ephemeral displays of pot-grown color will give freshness to the garden's design.

Trailing vegetables, such as tomatoes, cucumbers, peppers, or zucchini, are attractive in clay pots and can be supplemented with herbs, such as sage and marjoram, for winter interest or with flowers for sum-

mer color. Standard bays, gooseberries, vines, or hops trained on formal frames add grace to a circular tub or a square Versailles case. A fig will enjoy the restricted root conditions of a container, if it is placed in a sheltered position. Hanging baskets can be filled with cherry tomatoes, parsley, or herbs such as marjoram, thyme, or small-leaved sage. Strawberry barrels—tall earthenware pots with planting pockets at different levels—are plant containers *par excellence* for the kitchen garden. They keep the fruit clean and clear of the ground and are easy to net against birds.

TENTS, TEPEES, AND OBELISKS

The need to give support to climbing vegetables provides many opportunities for decorative structures in the garden. Most climbing vegetables are annuals and may be sown in a different place each year if some form of crop rotation (see p. 142) is being followed. The structures need to be designed so that they can be taken apart and then reassembled in a

(continued on p. 113)

Le Manoir de Criqueboeuf,
Normandy, France

MRS. YUL BRYNNER

The kitchen garden at Criqueboeuf is notable for its ingenious use of decorative fencing—some permanent, some movable—used to divide the garden rooms.

The garden is entered through a garden house smothered in passionflowers. (In accordance with

Below: A wide grass path lined with rose beds runs down the center of the garden.

local tradition, its thatched roof has a line of *Iris tectorum* along its ridge; by absorbing rainwater, the rhizomes help keep the roof dry.) A broad grassy path lined with box-edged rose beds runs down to the center of the garden where 8-foot-high clipped obelisks of yew rise out of platforms of clipped box. Grass paths, quiet and comfortable to walk on, are the most luxurious surface for a kitchen garden.

Left: The garden is subdivided by panels of locust-wood lattice that support a mixture of climbing vegetables and climbing roses.

Right: Low wire fencing supports tomatoes, while plaited layers of straw act as mulch for the strawberries in this well-crafted garden.

However, they are suitable only for large gardens, because they must be wide or they will suffer from wear.

The four quarters of the garden are subdivided by shoulder-high panels of locust-wood trelliswork, used to support climbing roses and beans. With their open construction, they suggest rather than actually define enclosure. Because the locust-wood panels can be disassembled and taken away at the end of each season, they can be re-erected the following season in a different location if desired. Further small-scale subdivisions are marked by waist-high wire fencing that supports tomatoes and dahlias. The wiring is attached to white-painted posts, which give the entire garden its strong character. (The posts in a neighboring garden are painted black, giving it an equally distinctive character.) These space-dividers shelter beds filled with mixed flowers, fruits, and vegetables. American sweet corn grows alongside double dahlias, and artichokes are companied with sunflowers. The flowers are refreshingly bright, primary colors and give the garden a different character from the others presented here, which employ carefully calculated, pale tones.

Also remarkable in this garden is the outstanding craftsmanship with which everything is grown and tended. For example, the strawberry beds are mulched with beautifully plaited straw layers, keeping the fruit off the wet ground and clean for picking. Surrounded on two sides by a common laurel hedge and on another side by an 8-foot-high, plain concrete wall, this garden, devoid of architectural or stylistic pretension, has an honest approach and elegant craftsmanship that is rarely seen today. Although designed originally by the French landscape architect Jacques Prevosteau, the garden has been maintained since its inception by Jacques Bourgeois. A native of Normandy, he was for many years chauffeur to the great French gardener (and uncle of Mrs. Brynner), the late Vicomte de Noailles. From him, he was able to absorb the influence of many of the well-known gardens of Europe.

new location. They are usually built about 6 to 10 feet high, the height most climbing vegetables reach. They may be constructed of straight poles or bamboo canes lashed together securely.

Tents

In a double row, 8-foot bamboo canes or flexible poles are set in the ground 1 foot apart. They are then bent, crossed at the top, and tied securely to a horizontal cane laid along the V-shaped channel formed by the crossings. A common variation is to tie the canes in groups of four. Runner beans, for example, can be set to climb up each cane.

Tepees

To make an isolated focal structure at the center of a bed or at each of the four corners, construct a tepee by setting eight to ten canes in a circle, perhaps 6 feet in diameter, and bend and tie them together about 6 inches from the top. A variation, often seen in Italy and gaining popularity in the United States, is to cross and tie the canes about halfway up their height.

Tripods

A three-pole tepee of approximately the same dimensions as the cane tepee above is strong enough to support the heavier climbing vegetables such as summer and winter squashes. Quadripods, an interesting four-pole variation, are often used in English National Trust gardens to support grapevines or hops grown to add height to an herb garden or a flower border.

Obelisks

Lightly constructed trelliswork obelisks can be put together in sections so that they are easy to dismantle and reassemble. They can be used to support a runner bean crop that can be rotated from one bed to another each year. Because they are decorative, they can be used as year-round focal points. Trelliswork has been a feature in gardens since ancient times, and many models for it can be found in the pages of garden history.

ORNAMENTAL FENCES AND CAGES

Low frames to train dwarf fruit or support tall vegetables can be used to form either permanent or temporary divisions within the garden. They can also be used to form a small room, or a corridor, or even a series of

Lady Rothschild's "bean fence" is constructed of rustic poles and galvanized wire.

architectural spaces. Depending on what kind of support is required, they can be constructed of wire mesh, of wooden lattice, or of horizontal or vertical wiring.

Climbing-Vegetable Fences

Four-foot-high lattice, recommended for fencing as early as the seventeenth century, is best suited for supporting twining climbers such as beans and peas. Latticework can be constructed with square or rectilinear patterns or with interesting diamond patterns. For more sophistication, try lattice in a *chinoiserie* pattern. The lattice panels can be supported on movable metal or wooden posts, which can themselves be decorated with balls or finials on top and moldings below. In one English garden, the timber posts are decorated on top with carved apples, pears, and other fruit. The whole assembly can be rearranged each year to suit the garden's current aesthetic: it might be in a zigzag or Greek key pattern, in a simple line, or in the form an enclosure. Instead of lattice or wire mesh, similar fences can be made up of woven willow or hazel hurdles.

Tall-Vegetable Fences

Fences to support tomatoes or Jerusalem artichokes, for example, must also be light and movable to follow the crop's rotation from year to year. However, they should not be constructed of lattice or mesh, but in panels of vertical wire (the wires 1 foot apart and the panels 6 feet high).

Fruit Fences

Because fruit trees and bushes are semipermanent plants, the fences they need for support are designed, unlike vegetable fences, to be permanent installations. However, the range of ornament and decoration used is similar. The panels that make up the fences should contain horizontal wiring (black-coated wiring is the least obtrusive) stretched between vertical posts. Against these wires, tree fruit can be espaliered and bush fruit trained.

CLOCHES, TUNNELS, AND FORCING JARS

Although it is possible to have a perfectly satisfactory vegetable garden without getting involved in the labor-intensive processes of forcing out-of-season fruit and vegetables, there is often a temptation to do so. There is a wide range of paraphernalia available for this purpose, and much of it, if well thought out and designed, can provide extra decorative elements for the garden.

Cloches

These are transparent glass, plastic, or polyethylene covers placed over a section of garden soil to warm it and so speed seed germination. In a cold climate, this is usually done two weeks before sowing. After the seed has germinated, the cloche can be retained for a while if the crop being raised is tender.

Glass Cloches

The traditional glass cloches have many advantages over the modern plastic variety. If kept clean, they let in more light. They retain more heat on a cold, clear night. They are more stable than those made of lighter materials in a wind-prone site. Unfortunately, they are expensive to buy and there are inevitable breakages.

 1. Lantern Cloches: These are an ancient form of cloche for forcing individual plants. They are constructed of small glass panes fitted into a lead or metal framework in the shape of a lantern. The roof can be lifted off for ventilation by means of a heavy metal ring. Some are square on cross section, others octagonal. All varieties are elegant as well as functional, but they are now considered garden antiques, and if they can be found at all, they are expensive.

2. Bell Cloches: The product of nineteenth-century improvements in glass technology, these bell-shaped, molded glass domes are crowned with a spherical knob for removing the top. Introduced to England by William Robinson, author of *The English Flower Garden* (John Murray, 1883), after he had seen them at the Paris Exhibition of 1867, they have the advantage of being lighter and therefore easier to move than the traditional leaded cloche.

3. Tent Cloches: Though more functional than elegant, these are visually very acceptable in an ornamental kitchen garden, provided they are kept clean. Formed of 2- by 1-foot panels of glass fixed at the top with a patent, galvanized-iron clip, they form a miniature glass tent about 12 inches high and 9 inches wide. The restricted height makes it suitable only for raising seedlings or for forcing single rows of low-growing vegetables like lettuces, carrots, or beetroots.

4. Low Barn Cloches: These are also more functional than elegant, made of four rather than two panes of glass, and held together by a wire frame rather than a simple clip. They enable spreading vegetables such as melons to be forced. Being 2 feet wide and 1 foot high, they will cover more than one row of vegetables: two rows of carrots or beetroots with a catch crop of lettuces in between.

5. High Barn Cloches: At 19 inches high, these are suitable for protecting tomatoes, eggplants, and peppers to advanced growth; they can be removed when the threat of frost has passed.

Plastic Cloches

Cheaper than glass, more expensive than polyethylene, and with a greater life expectancy than both, these are so light to handle that they can be up to 6 feet in length (a dimension that would be far too heavy and cumbersome to handle in glass). They are, however, available in a range of sizes stretching

Above: In Lady Rothschild's garden, a row of terra-cotta jars stands ready for blanching the sea kale recently planted in front.

from small individual units to continuous tunnels. Their width can vary from 1½ inches (designed to cover seedlings) to 2½ feet (which will cover two to three rows of vegetables). Their height varies from 4 inches for covering seedlings to 15 inches for pro-

tecting full-grown bush tomatoes, for example. They can be obtained with straight sides or curved into looped tunnels, the most common materials being polyvinyl chloride (PVC), polypropylene, or clear polystyrene.

Polyethylene Cloches

These are primarily used for forcing whole rows of plants. The polyethylene tunnels are supported on wire hoops so they may have limited use in a small domestic kitchen garden. Their lightness makes them flexible and easy to move from of one crop to another, but a disadvantage is that unless polyethylene cloches are regularly ventilated, condensation will form quickly on the inside, creating ideal conditions for fungal spread. The thinnest polyethylene available, 150 gauge, will last only a year or two, whereas the more expensive 500 gauge will last three to four years with care.

Cheesecloth Cloches

For those who like to use only organic materials in their gardens, opaque cheesecloth supported on bent hazel rods or light bamboo canes will provide an elegant and practical substitute for polyethylene.

Forcing Jars

These are tall, handsome terra-cotta jars, like old-fashioned chimney pots, with decorative caps and moldings. They are placed over rhubarb plants and also sea kale to blanch the tall stems. Used in lines or clusters in many old kitchen gardens, they form a decorative focal point.

WIT IN ORNAMENT

In many kitchen gardens, scarecrows and topiary figures offer evidence of the gardeners' sense of humor. To deter birds, scarecrows must be moved at intervals to different locations within the garden, and therefore they must be light and easy to handle. They can be made and dressed with invention, and in some instances, with success, they reach the elevated status of vernacular art objects. The scarecrows at Les Quatre Vents in Canada and at Glin in Ireland are good examples.

Topiary has been a decorative adjunct to gardens since classical times. Topiary has assumed many different, often elevated, architectural styles, but the kind of topiary appropriate to a kitchen garden should reflect a more domestic character. Sitting hens, ducks with dogs to protect them, fat elephants, or a Paddington Bear, like the one at Hillbarn House in England, which is fitted with with a newspaper and spectacles on garden open days, seem to embody the correct approach. Topiary carried out in clipped bay trees is in keeping with the concept of a kitchen garden, because its clippings can be saved and used by the cook.

Planting

Designing with
Fruits and Vegetables

Gilbert and Sullivan, in their opera *Patience,* wrote of a character who was "content with a vegetable love." Although characters with such a strong commitment to vegetables may be difficult to find, it can be argued that vegetable gardening is on the increase today because it meets deep emotional needs. People want to return to interacting with the natural world, and, by being involved from gardening to cooking to eating, to control what is going into their bodies. Kitchen gardening has become part of a new lifestyle. Mail-order catalogs no longer show gardeners in dirty overalls grubbing around in the dirt with a range of rudimentary tools. Now, they are depicted as elegant sophisticates, tending the soil in stylish garb, handling the

Left: At the Chateau de Villandry, Loire Valley, France, strength of design is achieved by restricting the planting of each bed to one vegetable only.

finest English gardening tools, and gathering the garden's harvest in hand-woven baskets or authentic Sussex trugs. In every magazine, food is celebrated in its uncooked as well as its cooked state. With the current elevated state of vegetables as food plants, the kitchen garden is no longer relegated to the back yard. In fact, it is finally being realized that

vegetables can be planted to give all the visual pleasure usually associated with a flower garden.

The secrets of designing with fruit and vegetables are similar to those used with conventional ornamental plants. Fruit trees and bushes take the place of the more conventional trees and shrubs. Climbing fruit and vegetables are used instead of the usual climbing flowers. Perennial and annual vegetables replace perennial and annual flowers. A principal difference, however, is in the proportion of each category of plant. In conventional gardens, most of the plants are long-

Below: At Barnsley House, Gloucestershire, England, the planting of each bed is deliberately restricted to two, sometimes three, vegetables. Combinations are chosen for the boldest effects from color and form.

Right: Designing with small plants is an exercise in the design of repeat patterns, as in the vegetable garden at Barnsley House.

lived trees, shrubs, and perennials, whereas in the kitchen garden, a preponderance of the plants are annuals—vegetables that are sown, grown, and harvested each year. Another difference is that a kitchen garden usually incorporates a greater range of plants within a given space and, on the whole, plants that are smaller than in the conventional garden. This demands very *tight* planning, often on a miniature scale. The small size of the individual plants demands their massing in large blocks or in bold and vivid combinations for maximum visual impact. At Villandry and at the garden of Mme. de Bagneux, both in France, strength of design is achieved by restricting the planting of each bed to one vegetable only. At Barnsley in England, the planting of each bed is restricted to two or three vegetable types, and even then it is carried out only in the boldest combinations of color and form. (Restricting the planting in this way has the practical advantage that the growing conditions, such as soil and height, can be geared precisely to the needs of one particular vegetable, or a limited combination, resulting in better yields.)

Designing with small plants, such as vegetables, *en masse* is an exercise in the design of repeat patterns: many individual plants being combined to form larger

(continued on p. 128)

Left: Regular and well-ordered vegetable patterns can be enhanced by occasional banks of flowers as at Lady Mary Keen's garden, St. Mary's Farm, Berkshire, England.

Te Doom, Veerlen, The Netherlands

Mrs. Ineke Greve

The kitchen garden at Te Doom is divided into quarters, each of which is planted to a separate theme. There is a strawberry garden, an herb garden, a salad garden, and a brassica garden. In the strawberry garden, the beds are edged with both alpine and variegated varieties. The beds are filled with a collection of no less than seventeen different strawberry varieties, including ones whose fruit is black, pink, or white, and ones whose flavor is pineapple or raspberry. Focal points are appropriately in the form of glazed strawberry pots punctuated with soil-filled openings planted with dwarf strawberry varieties. This is truly a garden for the strawberry connoisseur!

The brassica garden is filled not only with the succulent foliage of the cabbages, but also with other large-leaved crops like rhubarb, melon, and squash, giving this corner of the garden a luxuriant, subtropical atmosphere. In the salad garden, the dusky foliage of many bronze-leaved varieties of lettuce give an unusually somber and metallic look, but this is brightened by edgings of pink-flowered nasturtiums, chosen to match the color of Mrs. Greve's china when they are served in salads. The herb garden is the most complex in concept, because it is further subdivided into quarters.

A semiglazed strawberry pot planted with dwarf varieties is the focus of the strawberry garden, in which no fewer than seventeen different varieties are grown.

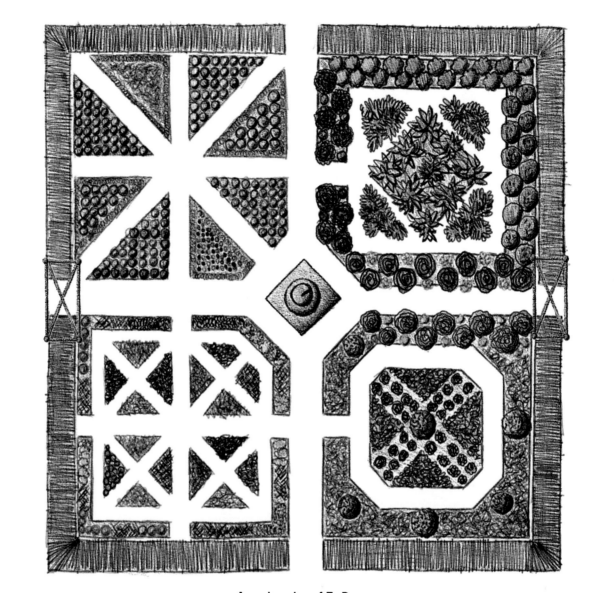

A garden plan of Te Doom.

One quarter is a thyme garden; it has many varieties with different scents and tastes. Another is an onion garden with chives, Egyptian and salad onions, and elephant and Chinese leeks ('Ciboule de Chine'). The last quarter is a garden devoted to leafy herbs like chervil, celery, and fenugreek.

In this view, the salad garden with its nasturtiums and purple-leaved lettuces is framed by a pair of standard apples being trained to a goblet form.

The garden is laid out in a traditional cross plan. Brick paths 2½ feet wide divide it into four, 23-foot-square quarters. The bricks, recycled from the demolitions of a number of old Dutch houses, are intriguingly colored. Work began five years ago and was mostly carried out by Mrs. Greve's son, a medical student keen to supplement his pocket money, together with the husband of a woman in her employment. As each load of bricks became available, Mrs. Greve would lay out a section of her path pattern in an evening and the following morning her son would set it permanently in mortar.

A diagonally set sundial forms a focal point at the center of the paths' crossing. A second focus is provided by a Regency seat under an arbor at one end of the garden. Located down a path lined with purple 'Drumhead' cabbages (called Cabbage Lane by Mrs. Greve), this seat is painted a stunning cobalt blue to pick up the glaucous blue and vinous purple tones of the cabbage leaves, as well as the brilliant blue of the morning glory flowers that cover the arbor. Glazed Portuguese and Spanish pots, some planted with decorative Japanese cabbages, are set informally along

Right: The hornbeam hedge and archway are clipped to a soft rounded outline. The herb garden's fine foliage in the foreground contrasts with the large leaves of the squashes in the garden behind.

the paths to provide subsidiary focal points for the eye should it become restless from wandering over the garden's intricate plantings.

As in many Dutch gardens, the *ensemble* is enclosed by high hornbeam hedges. These confine the view and encourage the inward focus on the subtle and intricate patterns and thematic planting that characterize the Dutch gardening tradition.

visual units—squares, triangles, circles, serpentines, chevrons, spirals, or a host of other possible forms. Complex patterns can be devised by arranging a number of different vegetables in repeating series, perhaps in alternate rows or blocks, interwoven units, or random tapestries. In most cases, each individual plant retains its distinct form while at the same time contributing to the overall pattern. Cabbages, leeks, corn, and butterhead lettuces are most effective in this style. In some cases, the individual plant loses its separate identity in the overall pattern of foliage. Fennel, asparagus, and carrots are good examples. Still others, like peas, beans, and potatoes, have undistinguished foliage and a rambling habit; they need a strong architectural framework to bring them into visual relief.

A secret of good kitchen garden design is that a regular and well-ordered vegetable pattern should be broken by the random self-sown flower or vegetable. At Barnsley in England, for example, an occasional hollyhock or mullein from the adjoining flower garden seeds itself into one of the vegetable beds and is allowed to remain to relieve the geometry of the rest of the planting. Russell Page, the great

modern garden designer, recommends the use of lamb's lettuce for this purpose: "a sprinkling of its seeds in the garden and you will never be without it since it seeds itself and has the odd habit of moving about the garden and appearing in unexpected places."

A theme can bring strong character to a garden. One garden might be designed to contain heirloom fruits and vegetables—historic varieties that have ceased to be generally cultivated. Such a garden is maintained at The Apprentice House, Quarry Bank Hill, Cheshire, England. A passion for Mexican food might suggest a garden, or a corner of one, devoted entirely to growing tender Mexican vegetables. Likewise, an interest in Oriental cuisine might lead to the creation of a garden devoted to the cultivation of Chinese vegetables, perhaps ones that are difficult to obtain in the grocery store. A gardener with cosmopolitan tastes living in an area that enjoys a mild climate might design a garden with sections labeled "Mexico," "Provence," "Italy," and "Japan," devoted to only those fruits and vegetables associated with the cooking of those regions.

Once a good kitchen garden planting has been created, it has to be maintained in good order. One secret is to keep, in a discreet position in the garden, a reserve bed for spare plants that can be used through the year to fill gaps that appear in the main planting. For example, holes that appear among win-

(continued on p. 133)

La Coquetterie, Normandy, France

M. AND MME. ADALBERT DE BAGNEUX

The modern technique of close planting for increased production as well as visual impact is well demonstrated in the kitchen garden of La Coquetterie. Its design is deceptively simple—thirty-six 2-meter-square beds in three rows of twelve each, with 1½-meter gravel paths between.

Only a light rustic fence separates it from the cattle yard, so there are some delightful pictures of cows looking over the fence at the vegetables. In each

Shrubs like this golden-leaved currant are chosen for their ability to survive severe pruning without losing vigor.

Of the thirty-six beds only six are devoted to vegetables and seven to edible herbs. The remainder are filled with shrubs for winter effect or with flowers like these tall irises for cutting.

bed, the plants of one variety are placed so close together that the effect is of a solid block of foliage color. Each bed's color is prevented from blending with the neighboring block of color by the wide gravel path between. When viewed from above, the effect is like looking into an enormous paint-box—a design idea first conceived by the great English garden designer Russell Page.

The garden is not entirely devoted to edible plants, and it could, at any time, revert to being

dedicated to flowers. In fact, out of a total of thirty-six beds, only six are devoted to vegetables and another seven to edible herbs. The remainder are planted with flowers for cutting, or shrubs for winter effect. The flowers are all tall-stemmed varieties of iris, daylily, salvia, hosta, and chrysanthemum used in the house for floral arrangements. The flowering shrubs are chosen for their ability to withstand severe and constant pruning without losing vigor—forsythia, perovskia, santolina, lavender, spiraea, and the golden-leaved currant. Other shrubs are chosen for their winter stem color—dwarf barberry, willow, and dogwood. Occasionally, carpeting conifers—dwarf spruce, cryptomeria, and microbiota—are used to give solidity of effect in winter. A raised stone edge around each bed serves to contain the frequent top-dressings of manure. The manure ensures the soil is a rich, dark, almost black color, which, when the beds are empty, adds its own contribution to the design, contrasting effectively with the pale adjoining gravel.

Unlike most kitchen gardens, the Bagneux's is not protected by a fence or wall. The aesthetic advantage derived from its openness is counterbalanced by the need to erect low chickenwire fences around some of the individual beds to protect the vegetables from rabbits. Supported on light, wooden, T-shaped

Below: A raised stone edge contains the top-dressings of manure that are applied to the beds. Aesthetically, they define the series of flat planes that characterize the garden's design and recall pre–World War II modernist schemes.

Right: Because the garden is not enclosed, low chickenwire fences supported on T-shaped stakes protect the lettuces from rabbits.

Three rows of twelve beds—each bed containing only one plant variety—give the effect of an enormous paint-box when they are viewed from above.

stakes, they are, however, very discreet and hardly noticeable except at close quarters.

The English garden tradition—in which the overall design is enriched by the seemingly casual detail or intricate plant combination designed to be enjoyed at close quarters—is not evident here. The French tradition of order and logic to achieve a bold and uncompromising overall picture triumphs. This garden was designed by Pascal Cribier, one of France's outstanding contemporary designers, who has recently been charged with the task of reorganizing Paris's famous Tuileries Gardens.

PLANTING TECHNIQUES AS AIDS TO DESIGN

Block Planting

One of the most fundamental changes in vegetable growing in recent years has been from the row system to the block system of planting. The widely spaced rows of the traditional kitchen garden resulted in fierce competition between the tightly set plants in each row for the limited nutrients, moisture, and available sunlight. Yet in the wide spaces between these rows, weeds flourished and competed with the vegetables for nourishment. The resultant vegetables were poor and of uneven shape and size.

In the modern block-planting system, vegetables are planted in staggered rows, and there is an equal distance between the plants in all directions. When mature, each plant's foliage just touches that of its neighbors, forming a weed-suppressing canopy over the soil. This is usually referred to as "close-planting."

ter greens by midsummer can be filled either with spares from the reserve bed or with a catch crop of kohlrabi, late lettuce, or spinach beet. The disadvantage this technique, however, is that it may weaken the overall design.

Intercropping can also be planned for aesthetic effect, as in the garden of Mudd's Restaurant in California.

Close-Planting

Traditionalists argue that close-planting must reduce a vegetable crop's yield. In fact, the reverse has been conclusively shown. Although the individual vegetables are smaller, crops are heavier. This is an advantage at a time when individual families are smaller but their diet more varied. (Indeed, nurserymen are deliberately breeding small vegetable varieties in response to today's market.) Spacing need not be standardized: it can be used as a tool to control the size, quality, and maturation time of vegetables to suit the individual grower's requirements. For example, close spacing of onions will produce small picking onions; moderate spacing, small cooking onions; and wide spacing, large onions. Tomatoes mature earlier and the quality of calabrese heads and self-blanching celery stalks improve with close spacing. The same principle holds true for carrots, cabbages, leeks, and many other vegetables. In fact, crops such as carrots, usually thinned to provide an initial harvest of early, tender vegetables, are indeed subjects for this close-planting technique.

The most extreme example of close spacing is in the growing of seedling crops—plants that are sown so close together that they do not develop beyond the seedling stage. However, this is just the moment when some crops are most delicious and nutritious. After they are cut and eaten once, they will usually grow again to give a second crop. In fact, with seedling crops like mustard, cress, salad rape, and fenugreek, several cuts can normally be made from one sowing. Golden purslane and the Japanese spring chrysanthemum are other crops that will remain leafy if picked frequently to keep them compact. Such close spacing is an aid to good design, because the densely growing foliage, with little or no soil visible between the plants, makes a strong visual impact.

PLANNED CROPPING

No matter how harmoniously vegetable patterns are arranged, there comes a time when they have to be cropped and eaten. To ensure that the ornamental quality of the garden is not lost during this process, it is as essential to crop to a pattern as it is to plant to one. If a bed of ornamental lettuces is cropped at random, it will look patchy and disorganized from the beginning to the end of the cropping season, and the appearance of the entire garden will be affected. If, however, it is cropped to a plan, it will retain a visual order throughout.

The center lettuce, for example, might be cropped first, followed by the plants surrounding it and so on in ever-widening circles until the plants around the perimeter of the bed are finally reached and cropped. As the cropping proceeds, the empty

(continued on p. 138)

Les Quatre Vents, Quebec, Canada

MR. AND MRS. FRANK CABOT

Because the main kitchen garden at Les Quatre Vents is located some distance from the house, Mrs. Cabot has made a more easily accessible salad and herb garden next to her kitchen. Its successful design and planting are inspirations for this type of spacing adjustment.

This garden consists of one raised bed, 18 inches above the ground, that is 20 feet long and 5 feet wide. It is divided by interior walls into three sec-

tions. Each section is planted in the form of an interlace or knot pattern reflecting one of Mrs. Cabot's other interests—textiles and their patterns. Lettuces in variety, baby carrots, corn salad, dill, and nasturtiums, are the basic plants here. The plants are not only arranged in a pattern, but they are also cropped to a pattern so as to keep an attractive display during the process of cropping. The basic cropping rules followed are:

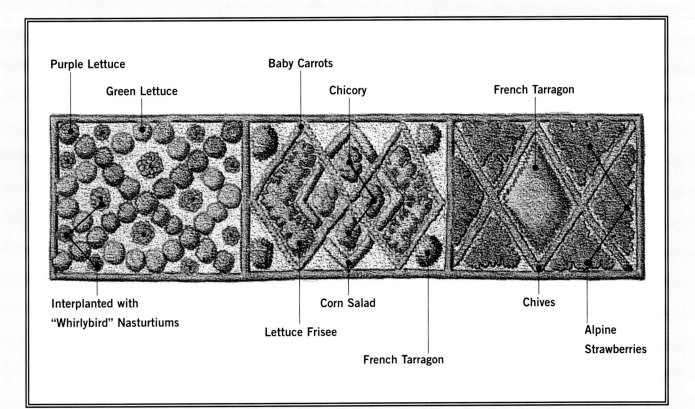

Purple Lettuce

Green Lettuce

Baby Carrots

Chicory

French Tarragon

Interplanted with
"Whirlybird" Nasturtiums

Corn Salad

Lettuce Frisee

French Tarragon

Chives

Alpine
Strawberries

a. Crop the outside leaves of lettuces first, allowing the inner head of the lettuce to fill out slowly.

b. When they are young, crop each alternate carrot plant; the vacant spaces created will be filled by the remaining carrot plants as they grow to maturity.

c. Crops like corn salad should be picked first when young so that they will continue to produce a succession of foliage through the summer.

An ongoing dilemma for the kitchen gardener is presented by vegetables that flower, or bolt, in an ornamental manner. At Highgrove, England, the majority of the lettuce is cropped and eaten, but a few plants in prominent positions are allowed to remain so that they can bolt into their typical cone shape and provide a vegetable ornament to the garden. At Sudborough Old Rectory, many of the beds are edged with chives. Some of them are clipped for use in the kitchen, but others are allowed to flower to decorate the garden. So as to keep the edgings thick and compact, those plants that were clipped one year are allowed to flower the next. At Barnsley, the chive edgings are clipped even more than normally required for the kitchen so as to maintain a constant supply of tender young leaves, which are tastier than the mature ones. At Barnsley also, occasional chicory plants are left in the ground to flower among the succeeding crop and break the formality of its ordered rows. In other gardens, bed edgings of sage are left unclipped in an occasional year, so they can produce their multitude of decorative blue flowers. A few plants of dill, fennel, or coriander are also sometimes left uncropped so that they flower and produce seed for later use in the kitchen.

Opposite: Undercropping: limited space can be maximized by raising vegetables under standard fruit trees, as at Barnsley House.

spaces can be filled with a new catch crop, perhaps a lettuce variety whose color contrasts with that of the main crop.

In the garden of Villandry, a different procedure is followed: each bed of vegetables is grown to a point of perfect maturity and then cropped in its entirety; those plants that are not eaten immediately are either frozen for later use or distributed locally. At Sudborough Old Rectory in England, red- and white-stemmed chard are planted alternately. When cropping time comes, the white chard is pulled first leaving behind a dazzling bed of red chard to await a second cropping. These are just some of the many

At Stavordale Priory, Somerset, England, a simple board walk is used to prevent soil compaction during resowing.

inventive ways of cropping vegetable beds so that the cropping itself becomes an integral part of the designing process.

Intercropping

Many vegetables grow slowly and occupy the full space allotted to them only after several months. While they are still growing, it is possible to grow a fast-growing crop between them, to be harvested and eaten long before the slow-growing crop matures.

Intercropping is usually carried out for increased productivity, but it can also be planned for aesthetic effect. Fascinating contrasts of color and form can be planned with the two crops. Bright green lettuce, for example, makes a vivid contrast grown among

At Barnsley House, beds awaiting a new main crop serve as
temporary seed beds.

blue-green leeks. Fast-growing, bright green lettuce
contrasts vividly with purple cabbage, purple brussels sprouts, or blue-green leeks.

Color harmonies, as well as color contrasts, can be
created. Purple-leaved lettuce will make a harmonious background for salsify's purple flowers, for yellow-green butterhead lettuce, or for the yellow flowers of scorzonera. Leeks and cabbages, when interplanted, can give subtle blue harmonies in addition
to their obvious contrast in form.

The Chinese—because of their space shortage—
have always used the intercropping technique. Their
traditional combination of bok choy with big, late-
cropping carrots can be converted to a decorative
combination: for example, if the bok choy is the purple variety with yellow flowers, it will contrast effec-

tively with the feathery green plumes of the carrot.
Likewise, their conventional interplanting of mustard and cabbage becomes exciting if the purple-
leaved mustard is chosen to contrast with the cabbage variety 'Eskimo', whose inner leaves are yellow-
white. The gardener with an experimental turn of
mind will enjoy planning new combinations to
achieve decorative effects.

To save space, the Chinese also practice another
form of intercropping, commonly called the relay
system, in which a new crop is planted alongside a
crop waiting to be harvested. By the time the new
crop needs space, the first crop will be gone. Of
course, the system can also be practiced for aesthetic effect as well as for productivity.

It is important to remember that if intercropping
is practiced frequently without adding nourishment
back to the soil, the slow-maturing main crop will
suffer when the soil becomes depleted.

Undercropping

Advantage can be taken of the wide variety of vegetables that thrive when planted low or trailing, under and between tall or climbing varieties. The practical advantage of this technique is that the trailing plants provide a weed-suppressing groundcover under the taller ones. The aesthetic appeal is that the use of tall and climbing vegetables is an ideal way of introducing contrasting form and height to the garden's inherently low profile.

Sweet corn is an ideal subject for undercropping, as its stems stand well upright and its foliage casts only a light shade. Many plants are suitable as undercrops. The Japanese mustard 'Mizuna', for example, will continue to provide fresh cuttings long after the sweet corn has been harvested. Other successful undercrops are trailing vegetables (squash, gherkins, and cucumbers), summer herbs (parsley, marjoram, savory, and basil), and compact plants (dwarf beans and lettuces). The design-conscious gardener will want to try purple basil and lettuce under sweet corn's red, purple, or black forms; or tall, purple brussels sprouts underplanted with harmonizing purple basil or contrasting golden marjoram; or feathery-leaved asparagus underplanted with a contrasting, smooth-leaved lettuce.

Climbing vegetables like peas and beans growing on tents or tepees can be underplanted with a quick-

Hens make an unexpected "undercrop" in the orchard of Hope End Hotel, Herefordshire, England.

In the de Belders's kitchen garden in Belgium, the squash crop is elegantly displayed on a grass bed in a wheelbarrow

Catch Cropping

Conventional vegetable gardening often leaves beds lying fallow for part of the year. This is not only a poor use of valuable space but an affront to the eye. The use of a fast-maturing catch crop, either before or after the main crop, will not only make the ground more productive but keep it looking attractive as well.

Early catch crops, such as small carrots, beetroots, lettuces, spring onions, spinach, and oriental vegetables, can be sown and harvested before planting out, in the same bed, the main later-season crops of brussels sprouts, winter cauliflower, spring cabbage, sweet corn, or tomatoes. A popular cropping sequence is the sowing of 'Tom Thumb' lettuce in March as a catch crop after a winter crop of brussels sprouts has been harvested and before the planting of a tomato crop in June.

growing crop to be harvested before the former completely shades it. Herbs, lettuce, and dwarf varieties of peas and beans also make good undercrops. A visual treat is the reward for underplanting the purple-flowered and -podded French bean with purple basil or the yellow-podded bean with golden marjoram.

Typical late catch crops are dwarf beans, often planted to follow a crop of broccoli when it is harvested in May, or lettuce following a crop of spring cabbage. Rosemary Verey uses the latter at Barnsley. Harvesting the center of her bed of cabbages first, she immediately replants it with a bright green lettuce to contrast with the blue-green of the remaining cabbage. In due course, she replaces the last of the cabbage with a red lettuce to contrast with the bright green one already in place at the bed's center. Using the catch crop technique, she is able to achieve a succession of aesthetic effects.

Serial Cropping

One of the greatest challenges for the owner of a small vegetable garden is to ensure that there is a continuous succession of vegetables ready for eating. Nothing is more wasteful than to have a glut of vegetables for a short time, followed by an acute shortage (although this is sometimes unavoidable because of the vagaries of the weather). A continuous supply means sowing only short rows, perhaps 3 feet in length, of each vegetable at a time, then sowing again at two- or three-week intervals through the season. This approach is essential for vegetables like radishes that do not keep well, but it is also worthwhile for other fast-maturing crops like beetroot, carrots, spring onions, and spinach. Even for slower-growing crops it pays to plan a succession, although it will be more limited. A first sowing of dwarf beans is often made (under a cloche) in April, another in May or June, and a last one in July. Peas, carrots, brussels sprouts, and zucchinis are available in cultivars that mature at different times, so that a succession of produce can be arranged by planting early-, mid-, and late-season cultivars. Serial sowings or plantings made alongside each other in the traditional way never look attractive. With each row at a different stage of maturity, the result is visually confusing. It is much better for aesthetic appeal to incorporate each successive sowing as an intercrop among other vegetables.

Mixed Cropping

Gardeners who are not able to schedule frequent serial sowings can benefit from a new development—the mixed seed packet—in which several early-, mid-, to late-season vegetables are included. Some seed mixtures like "Misticanza," "Meselum," and "Saladini" contain up to a dozen different vegetables chosen to germinate in sequence over a twelve-month period. A long harvesting period can be achieved with a single sowing.

Of course, it is possible to make up a seed mix instead of using a ready-mixed packet. A good "salad cocktail" for year-round eating might include cress, Mediterranean rocket, chervil, 'Salad Bowl' lettuce, 'Sugar Loaf', and 'Red Italian' chicory. It is a surprise to learn that this is not a new idea, for John Evelyn, the seventeenth-century English diarist, recommended using such a mixture (lettuce, purslane, claytonia, carrots, radishes, and parsnips), all of which would come up in turn, with the parsnips lasting until winter. However, traditional undersowings are of a simpler, two-in-one kind—fast-germinating radish or 'Tom Thumb' lettuce among slower carrots, parsley, or parsnips. Fast-maturing spring onions with carrots have a peculiar advantage in that the smell of the onions, particularly during cropping, disguises that of the carrots and deters the carrot fly. Mixed sowings or plantings generate close-growing carpets of randomly distributed vegetables that act as an excellent visual foil for the ordered geometry of most kitchen gardens.

CROP ROTATION AND DESIGN

For those accustomed to conventional forms of gardening, the concept of crop rotation may be unfamiliar. It can be likened to the occasional requirement to move rose bushes or primulas because the soil in which they are growing has become exhausted of the particular nutrients required to grow them.

Crop rotation in a kitchen garden prevents the exhaustion of nutrients required for growing certain vegetables. If, rather than being considered a chore, this is viewed as a positive opportunity to experiment with new cropping patterns from year to year, crop rotation can become one of the biggest forces for exciting kitchen garden design.

Crop rotation has been practiced in some form since the Middle Ages. In those days, part of a garden's ground was left fallow every third year so that it could recover its fertility. Since then, crop rotation, which is a more economical system than fallowing, has gradually become more refined. Today, it is a principal factor in crop management.

Crop rotation requires being mindful of the different cultural needs of different vegetables. Some, such as peas and beans, require a rich soil. Root crops like carrots and parsnips do better in a soil that is less rich. The brassicas—cabbages, kales, and brussels sprouts—need a lime-rich soil. Vegetables can be grouped into beds according to their shared requirements, and the soil fertilized and manured as necessary. However, because each group of vegetables takes a different set of nutrients from the soil, repeated growing of one group in the same bed will result in a soil exhausted of those particular nutrients. Therefore it is well worth moving each group of vegetables from bed to bed every year.

Rotation also reduces the risk of disease. Each vegetable group has its own range of pests and diseases—the cabbage family is prone to club-root, the onion family encourages the eel-worm. Continual growing of one family in the same bed consolidates the hold of that family's pests and diseases on that bed. These can be reduced, however, if the family is moved on. Cabbage root fly, which attacks cabbages in one bed, will not attack root crops if they are planted in it the next year. The maggots of the pea moth will not affect a crop of brassicas in the same bed during the following year. However, rotation is not a foolproof method of avoiding trouble. Although it will deter less-mobile, below-ground pests like the eel-worm, which affects cabbages and potatoes, and it will reduce fungal attack from soil-borne spores, it will not be very effective in counteracting mobile, above-ground pests.

Crop Rotation in Practice

Crop rotation is easily adaptable to the needs of every garden. Some people may wish to practice it in a relaxed and informal way, as circumstances allow. Others will be more systematic, changing their crop locations each year according to a careful plan. The manner in which rotation is practiced also depends on the family's vegetable preferences. When devising a plan, remember that catch crops, because they are in the ground for such a short time, are usually not worked into the rotation scheme.

In the great estate gardens of the nineteenth century, a rotation on a complicated seven-year cycle ensured that club-root and the eel-worm (neither of which can survive in the soil longer than that period) were totally eliminated. Nowadays, a simpler five- or even a three-year cycle is usually implemented. This cycle is not sufficient to eliminate many pests and diseases, but it will bring them under control.

A typical three-year cycle for one of the garden's beds would be:

Year 1	Pulses and salads	Peas, beans, onions, leeks, lettuce, spinach, celery, tomatoes (Substantial quantities of manure are required for these heavy feeders, but the pulses will leave the soil nitrogen-rich, as they have the capacity to convert it from the air to a usable form.)
Year 2	Brassicas	Cabbages, cauliflowers, broccoli, kale, brussels sprouts (A lime-dressing for the soil is required before planting to prevent club-root disease.)
Year 3	Root crops	Carrots, potatoes, beetroot, parsnips, rutabagas (Too rich a soil will result in root deformation. The rich manure fed to the pulses and the salads in the first year will have broken down by this time to a fertile humus, which will need only a general fertilizer dressing before sowing.)

A more sophisticated five-year cycle for the garden's beds might be:

Year 1	Potato family	Potatoes, eggplants, tomatoes, peppers
Year 2	Pulses and salads	Peas, beans
Year 3	Brassicas	Cabbages, broccoli, kale
Year 4	Onions	Onions, leeks, garlic
Year 5	Umbellifers	Carrots, parsnips, parsley, celery

The challenge for the kitchen gardener is to capitalize on the necessity of crop rotation to produce an ornamental garden with interesting and unique designs. Whatever the overall size of the garden, it is easier to implement a rotation plan with many small individual beds than with one large plot. If the beds are all of the same size, crop rotation is easy, because a planting design for one bed can be rotated to another bed without thought in the following year. If, however, the beds are of different sizes, a different planting scheme has to be invented by the gardener for each year of the rotation. A plan with all of the beds of the same size need not be boring—a glance at the Sudborough Old Rectory garden shows that a garden does not need to be of rectangular units or even symmetrical.

Color, Form, and Texture
in the Kitchen Garden

To most people, garden color means flower color. But leaves also have color, usually more subtle and subdued, and it offers a powerful antidote to the shocking, man-made hues that dominate the world today. Most kinds of fruit and vegetables have a low-toned color, yet they posses an unexpected range of hues. Robert Carvalho, owner of the great vegetable garden of Villandry in France, writes, "The texture, shape and changing colors of vegetables allow both unusual decorative effects and unexpected harmonies." Indeed, some of the Japanese cabbage varieties being used by his wife in the garden have color as bright as any flowers. With the increasing popularity of kitchen gardens, nurserymen are releasing vegetables and fruits of increasingly

sequently be altered by its stage of growth or external conditions. Bright colors, for example, may look pale in strong sunlight but more colorful on an overcast day. Vegetables growing in the gray light of a northern garden, such as Les Quatre Vents in Canada, look different from the same vegetables growing in the ocher-colored soil and bluish foliage of the garden of Monticello in Virginia. Colors in the garden are even affected by the colors of nearby architecture. In short, it is possible to plan color in the garden, but not always to control it.

The simplest way of combining colors in the garden is to create either

arresting color—so much so that there has already been a backlash in some quarters in favor of the old, "unimproved" varieties.

It is not possible for a gardener to be as precise with a color scheme as a painter composing on a canvas. A gardener must work with the plant material available to him, the appearance of which will sub-

harmonies or contrasts. Harmony results when all the colors chosen share one pigment, allowing the eye to travel naturally from one to the other. Because vegetable foliage is not uniform but has a multiplicity of tints and shades, a kitchen garden can be planned with many different color harmonies. Consider, for example, the case of the cabbage 'Gray

Left: Planting for color contrast at Barnsley House— bright green sweet corn and dusky red lettuce.

Below: Scarlet-flowered nasturtiums trail through different-colored lettuces in the kitchen garden at Les Quatre Vents, Quebec.

Laird'. Its leaves are silvery and light-reflecting in the sun, but blue-green in the shade. The former property can be used in developing an all white-and-gray color scheme, and the latter can serve in a scheme of glaucous green and blue. Plant harmonies from similar colors are much easier to create than contrasts, which require using a combination of colors that do not share a common pigment. The result is that the eye needs to refocus as it moves from one color to the next. Dramatic and stimulating shifts of mood can be induced by inserting contrast into a planting scheme that is characterized by its quiet color harmonies. For example, an edging of marigolds is always very striking in a kitchen garden, because its orange flowers are in direct contrast with the blue-greens of brassicas, leeks, onions, and other vegetables.

Colors can be a tool to manipulate our sense of perspective. For example, they can be used to create the effect of increased or reduced garden space. Distance can be created visually by using plants with predominantly blue tones: sea kale, onions, chives,

(continued on p. 155)

COLOR, FORM, AND TEXTURE IN THE KITCHEN GARDEN **149**

Walnut Creek, California, United States

The key vegetable in the kitchen garden at Mudd's Restaurant is lettuce, which is used in many different colors and textures to create patterns of a precision and originality unexpect-

Below: A pre-dinner visit to the kitchen garden reassures the customers at Mudd's about the quality and freshness of the fruit and vegetables being served.

Opposite: Heartsease flowers show through low-espaliered apples in Lady Rothschild's garden.

Left: Red and green lettuce varieties make a chevron pattern as bright as any on a medieval banner.

Right: Newly planted lettuces create a *staccato* visual rhythm.

ed beyond the great French garden of Villandry. Red, bronze, and bright green varieties, for example, are grown in chevron patterns as bright as those on any medieval banner. The same plant combinations are also used to make diamond, lattice, and stripe patterns. The background of the pattern is sometimes the purple lettuces, sometimes the green ones. Frisée, oak-leaf, and butterhead varieties are used so that their different textures underline the color schemes. Elsewhere, combinations such as purple-leaved chicory with blue-leaved leeks create patterns equally precise and striking.

An interesting development in the contemporary presentation of vegetables at the table is the practice of serving whole vegetables rather than parts. A dwarf or baby carrot is preferred to slices of a standard one. A serving of whole, currant-sized tomatoes

Left: Shasta daisies, valerian, marigolds, and mulleins are grown for use in the restaurant's table arrangements.

Red, bronze, and bright green lettuce varieties are cropped as required to make interesting table salads.

An important part of food presentation is a table arrangement of flowers. Mudd's grows Shasta daisies, sweet williams, marigolds, and valerian as edgings around many of the vegetable beds. The flowers thus decorate the garden before they are picked to decorate the tables.

The best seafood restaurants keep fish in small aquariums as an assurance of freshness. The kitchen garden at Mudd's serves the same purpose for their fruits and vegetables. In fact, a pre-dinner visit to the garden is part of the evening's experience.

Designed to serve the needs of a restaurant rather than a family, the garden is larger and under more intensive cultivation than many in this book. There is much to learn from observing the details of its design, is thought to look better than slices of a larger tomato, regardless of how elegantly the latter are arranged. Vegetable breeders have responded by creating new varieties of dwarf fruit and vegetables, and, because food presentation is particularly important in their restaurant, Mudd's grows a wide range of them.

which was created and is still supervised by Rosalind Creasey, who lives south of San Francisco. Creasey is a prolific author on "edible landscaping," a concept she originated. Her best-known book, *Cooking from the Garden* (Sierra Club Books, 1988), is a combined garden and cookbook presenting vegetables and fruit from seventeen different theme gardens.

Silver-leaved artichokes, shown here at La Petite Fontanille, Provence, France, have immature flower buds, known as chokes, that are vinous red in color.

and brussels sprouts. On the other hand, distance can be shortened by using plants with warmer colors, such as ruby chard, beetroot, or purple-headed cabbage.

Depth of color can also alter how we perceive space. Pale colors, because of their peaceful, restful tones, lead the eye into the distance. By creating a diffused rather than a defined sense of space, they increase the apparent dimensions of a garden or its parts. For example, a path will appear to be wider if it is lined with hedges of pale-colored lavender, and it will appear to be narrower if it is lined with dark-colored box. The disadvantage of pale foliage, however, is that it can look dull from a distance and fade into insignificance in strong sunlight. When used in broad masses, it can lose any interesting architectur-

al or formal distinction it may have had, resulting in a kind of visual instability. These shortcomings can be counteracted by using occasional areas of darker foliage (the dark Irish yew stabilizes the muted colors of the garden at Stavordale Priory), richer color (the warm brick color of the paths at Barnsley and at Sudborough counteracts the cool, quiet foliage of the vegetables), or strong, architectural planting (such as globe artichokes, rhubarb, clipped hedging, or topiary). Despite the fact that pale shades and tints demand close attention if their subtlety is to be appreciated, they are easier to use with success than their stronger-toned counterparts.

Some vegetables have flowers, fruit, or foliage of vivid hues. Although it is easy to use them as accents in a bed of low-toned foliage, experience and courage are required to combine them. In a mixed bed, a balance can be achieved by using the principle of weighting: strong and dominant colors are better balanced with weaker ones if the former occupy less space. Strong color is recommended to emphasize a plant's form or architectural properties as part of the overall design. For example, in a cabbage bed, the purple variety 'Red Drumhead' might be used as punctuation in the corners of the bed that is otherwise planted with the standard green-leaved 'Christmas Drumhead'.

Color schemes should also take into account the color of building materials used in the nearby house, walls, or paving attached to the garden, as the pale-toned foliage of Stavordale Priory's garden harmonizes with the cool colors of the stone used in the construction of the house. Other important factors are the color of the local soil (which can vary from black through browns and reds to sandy) and the color of mulches (dark peat, farmyard manure, mushroom compost, forest bark, straw, or sawdust). The rich brown of the crushed cocoa shells used as a mulch at Barnsley alters the color balance of the planting. Soil and mulch colors are of special importance in the kitchen garden where, at certain times of the year, extensive areas of both may be clearly visible. Finally, any color scheme should take into account the garden's climate and geographic location. In a northern climate, for example, blues increase in intensity, but they look washed-out in a hotter, southern climate. Bright sunlight will make ordinary oranges and yellows look faded, which is why, in a tropical climate, the very brightest colors are needed.

Color can also be used according to personal choice. Some gardeners prefer to have no bright colors at all: stimulation is less important than subtle textural differences, and color is used to emphasize shape and form. Others choose to have color dictate the garden's style and its emotional effects, using reds to evoke a dramatic mood, or blues to soothe.

No matter what the intention, the effective use of any color depends on close planting to create the effect of solid sheets of color. Any color scheme will fail if the individual plants are too far apart to be "read" across the intervening patches of soil. This situation exists when young, slow-maturing vegetables are first planted out, but the effect in this case is easily minimized by planting a catch-crop of faster-maturing plants between the main crop seedlings. When plants are scattered singly or in small groups throughout the garden, the impact of their color is lost. The effectiveness of massing plants in a single block of color is demonstrated by Rosemary Verey's grouping of all her standard 'Iceberg' roses in the center of the kitchen garden at Barnsley rather than scattering them about. Another pitfall is the use of too many different colors, resulting in a spotty effect, which, particularly in a small garden, is visually restless and exhausting. One need not be limited to just a few colors, but it is important to be selective, combining colors in strong and purposeful associations, avoiding such a discreet use of color that no definite impression is made.

PLANT COLORS

The following color divisions are based not on the conventional color spectrum, but on the colors found in kitchen gardens. The lists of vegetables, herbs, and fruits in each section are not meant to be exhaustive, simply to suggest some of the possibilities open to the kitchen gardener.

White, Silver, and Gray

These colors have appeal in a garden because of their refreshing simplicity. They do not clash with neighboring colors but take on, to some degree, a hint of a companion color by reflection. White is often "shadowed" by a tint that is complementary to the neighboring color. For example, white flowers set against a background of dark yew are often tinged with complementary pink. Therefore, they are ideal colors to soften or separate already clashing plant associations.

WHITE, SILVER, AND GRAY vegetables

Artichoke	'Gros Vert de Leon'	A tall plant of strong architectural form, with silver foliage and purple flowers. It would not be out of place in a perennial border.
Broad bean	'The Sutton' (dwarf)	White flowers are followed by well-filled pods on dwarf plants that are ideal for the small garden.
Broccoli	'Regilio'	A variety with large, gray, dome-shaped flowerheads sitting on a bed of frost-gray leaves.
	'Improved White Sprouting'	A hardy over-wintering variety with creamy white flowerheads for cutting in spring.
Cabbage	'Greyhound'	An early-maturing variety with a compact but pointed head of distinctly gray foliage.
Cardoon	'Violetta di Chioggia'	With its silver foliage and purple flowers, it closely resembles the artichoke.
Cauliflower	'Snowball'	One of many varieties with pure white, solid heads, or curds.
	'Elby'	The easiest cauliflower to grow, with very large, dense white curds in a heavy leaf jacket.
Chinese cabbage	'China Pride'	These strong, erect plants have dark green leaves with broad mid-ribs that are pearly white.
	'Eskimo'	Its central leaves turn creamy white with maturity. The appearance of this white head is a sign that the plant is ready for harvesting.
Runner bean	'White Achievement'	Its white flowers are followed by long, slender pods of excellent flavor.
Swiss chard	'Lucullus'	Its abundance of large green leaves have wide white mid-ribs and provide a continuous supply of "greens" throughout summer and autumn.
Welsh onion		The white flowers of this perennial plant are displayed atop the edible fleshy leaf bases.

Very few fruits or vegetables have colors that are pure white. White gooseberries or raspberries, for example, are really cream in color. The white stems of Swiss chard are, in reality, ivory, and the young foliage of the Japanese cabbage 'Mizuma' is strongly tinged with pink.

Deliberate color accents can be created in the garden by planting whites, silvers, or grays against a dark background. The cream-and-white variegated strawberry is strongly delineated when set against a box hedge, for example. Conversely, white can be blended with a darker background color by introducing intermediary silvers and grays. Herbs like lavender, rosemary, and sage are ideal for this purpose in the kitchen garden. Their gray colors appear lighter or darker depending on the adjacent colors. The

Gooseberry	'Careless'	Large, smooth, milky green berries on a bush of upright growth.
	'Whitesmith'	Creamy colored berries on a bush of spreading habit.
White currant	'White Versailles'	The traditional variety producing large white berries with a sweet flavor.

WHITE, SILVER, AND GRAY herbs

Rosemary		Its grayish green aromatic leaves, which are used for flavoring, can be clipped into a hedge, an obelisk, or another formal shape to give year-round architectural form.
Sage		Growing with its gray-green leaves to a height of 2 feet, it can be kept clipped to a lower height as a bed edging.
Thyme	*Thymus lanuginosus*	This gray carpeter is used along border edges, in paving cracks, or for making small patches of lawn within the kitchen garden.

appearance of silver or gray foliage is very dependent on the form and texture of the leaves—whether they are rough or smooth, matte or shiny. An advantage of the gray-foliaged plants is that many are evergreen and make ideal structural planting, giving substance to the garden in winter when many of its vegetables have been cropped.

Yellows

Yellow, the color of sunlight, cheers the spirit. The most luminous of hues, it catches the eye more readily than any other color, and then it dominates all adjoining colors. In the same way that intense sunlight dazzles, yellow neutralizes visual depth, preventing clear perspective. A sense of detail is easily lost. Therefore, yellow is best used as a focal point rather than as the major color in a scheme. The stronger, acidic yellows can be toned down by com-

French bean pods are often splashed with crimson or maroon and ripen to a clear yellow.

binations with gray or gray-green foliage. Cream, pale gold, or lime-green foliage can also be used to subtly link clear yellows to surrounding greens. The pale green lettuce varieties 'Helian' or 'Lollo Bionda' are very useful in the kitchen garden for this purpose. In fact, many green leaves contain sufficient yellow tone to harmonize with yellow flowers, fruits, and foliage.

Yellows find their complementary colors in blues, mauves, and violets. Golden-podded beans work well

YELLOW vegetables

Broccoli	'Romanesco'	Its distinctive lime green–yellow curds are produced in late autumn. A gourmet's broccoli, exceeding all other varieties in flavor, it is widely grown in Italy.
Zucchini	'Gold Rush'	Prolific in fruit, this compact and bushy plant produces rich yellow flowers and deep yellow, slightly curved zucchinis.
Endive	'Croquette'	This is a selection of the superb French variety, 'Très Fine Maraichene'. Its finely cut, curled, yellow-green leaves tint to pale yellow at the center of the head.
French bean	'Wachs Goldperle'	A dwarf French bean sometimes known as a kidney bean. This one carries clusters of golden yellow pods and is highly esteemed by continental European cooks as its beans remain tender for a long time.
	'Belidor'	Its bright yellow pods are carried high on the plant, making them not only more visible, but also easier for picking.
Lettuce	'Lollo Bionda'	Many lettuce varieties have yellow-green leaves, but this variety has leaves of such a lime green–yellow color that it is suggested for use in yellow color schemes. It stands in the garden for a long period before bolting.
Summer squash	Burpee's 'Golden Zucchini'	These golden-skinned fruits, which can be used either as summer squash or zucchinis, should be cut often, as they are best when small and tender.
Okra	'Long Green'	Although okra is grown for its edible seed pods, its dark-centered yellow flowers are an ornament in the kitchen garden.
Pepper	'Luteus'	The large fruits can be harvested when green, or later, when they turn yellow in maturity.
Tomato	'Golden Sunrise'	These smooth, golden yellow tomatoes have a sweet, fruity flavor.
	'Golden Boy'	These globe-shaped, golden yellow tomatoes have a distinctive flavor.

YELLOW fruits

Alpine strawberry	(yellow)	Cropping all summer and autumn, this golden-fruited wild strawberry is ideal as an edging or in the pockets of shaded paving.
Apricot	'Moor Park'	This most popular variety has round, maize-yellow fruit that ripens at the beginning of August.
Greengage	'Oullins'	This tree of upright growth can be fan-trained against a wall; it bears sweet golden greengage fruit.
Gooseberry	'Laxton's Amber'	A compact, upright bush bearing small golden berries that are among the sweetest of their kind.
Crab apple	'Golden Hornet'	A compact, upright crab apple bearing an immense crop of golden fruit in October.
Pear	'Packham's Triumph'	Of upright, compact growth and similar to the most popular of all pears, 'William's Bon Chretien', with pale, golden yellow fruit.
Plum	'Pershore Egg'	This yellow, egg-shaped plum is a prolific and regular bearer.
Raspberry	'Golden Everest'	The best yellow raspberry, it fruits over a long season on both young and old canes.

YELLOW herbs

Dill		An annual with feathery, blue-green foliage, topped with small panicles of yellow flowers.
Fennel		A perennial, though often grown as an annual, its fine leaves are also topped with yellow flowers.
Golden marjoram		An annual with golden leaves, this herb is used to flavor meat, fish, and tomatoes.
Golden thyme	*Thymus* x *citriodorus* 'Aureus'	Its golden leaves make fine bed edgings.
Variegated lemon balm		This perennial has yellow variegation on its lemon-scented, heart-shaped leaves.

interplanted with purple-podded varieties. The mauve-to-violet flowers of chives, salsify, sage, or lavender make a complementary edging for a bed of yellow vegetables or fruit. The dull purple foliage of 'Red Drumhead' cabbage or purple-sprouting broccoli blend nicely with a bed of yellow tomatoes or peppers, or the yellow flowers of okra or scorzonera.

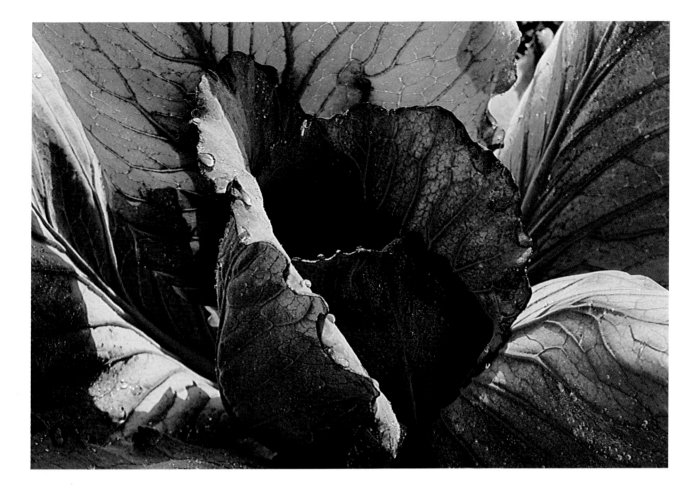

Blues

Unlike yellows, blues do not define dimension. Blues create a sense of distance, making gardens appear larger. On the other hand, this quality can affect a garden's sense of containment and security. Their overuse, except in a small garden, should be avoided.

Pure blue is rare in the plant world. Vegetable blues are, in the first place, rarely monochrome—the color of every leaf varies in shade. Further, most vegetable blues tend to be pale, luminous, and cool. Blueberries, loganberries, and black currants are among the few that are dark and glowing.

Colors linked by blue pigment blend into subtle "misty" pictures. The effect is more marked when the garden is viewed from a distance. Blue plants lose their individual identities and blend with each other in an undefined blue "haze."

Glaucous-blue leaves with purple venation characterize this red cabbage growing in the Shep Ogden garden in Vermont.

Gray-blue or glaucous foliage will brighten more somber purple blues—for example, sea kale interplanted with purple 'Drumhead' cabbage. However, an occasional complementary splash of ivory, cream, or yellow will make blues seem brighter (as was first suggested by Gertrude Jekyll). Variegated mint or cream-and-white variegated nasturtiums can be used as edgings around beds of blue Savoy cabbages, for example. Silver foliage will make adjoining blues seem deeper. The use of blues with their complementary orange, as in a bed of blue-leaved leeks surrounded by marigolds, makes a harsh contrast, better tolerated as an isolated incident than as the main feature.

BLUE vegetables

Brussels sprouts	'Bedford Asmer Monitor'	Its foliage, like that of many winter vegetables, has a bluish tinge. It is small, compact, and more elegant than the larger garden varieties.
	'Achilles'	Stands in the garden over five winter months providing both a long-lived ornament to the garden and a continuous crop for the table.
Cabbage	'Celtix'	A short-stemmed, ball-headed, blue-green variety that stands outdoors without spoiling until January or February.
Kale	'Westland Autumn'	An ornamental plant with tightly curled leaves providing winter and early spring "greens."
Kohlrabi	'Rolano'	A fast-maturing, blue-green vegetable with succulent, swollen stems that are ready for cutting eight weeks after sowing.
Leek	'Cortina'	With its dark blue-green leaves, this variety combines exceptional winter hardiness with long standing ability.
Onion	'Winter White Bunching'	Blue-green foliage grows from bulbs that are slow to form, but have good over-wintering ability.
Salad onion	'Ishekuro'	Blue-green grassy foliage on plants that are gradually thinned between spring and autumn to provide a long season of harvesting.
Savoy cabbage	'Wivoy'	Being highly frost resistant, this variety, with its deeply crimped, bluish, gray-green leaves, stands in the ground until April.
	'January King'	A hardy 'Drumhead'-type cabbage with a bluish tinge to its leaves.
Sea kale	'Lily White'	A hardy perennial with deep blue-green leaves that will crop for many years.

BLUE fruits

Blueberry	'Jersey'	This variety, one of many, carries short sprays of round blue berries that follow the white, heathlike flowers. The foliage turns a vivid scarlet in autumn.
Damson	'Farleigh Damson'	Round-to-oval, small, blue-black fruits are born, often in enormous crops, on this upright tree.
Plum	'Kirbe's Blue'	This small but spreading tree has tasty fruit with a heavy blue bloom.

BLUE herbs

Borage		An easy-to-grow annual; the leaves and blue flowers are used to flavor salads.
Rosemary		A blue-flowered evergreen shrub with fragrant gray leaves used for flavoring meat or fish dishes.

Pinks and Mauves

These quieter tints reassure the viewer of the essential restfulness of a garden environment, evoking a peaceful atmosphere absent from gardens dominated by the more lively blues, yellows, reds, and oranges. Self-effacing and undemanding, they make excellent background colors. However, they make up for their lack of impact with their delicacy and sophistication at close quarters. They assume a certain strength when used in association with silver foliage, a certain brilliance with gray foliage, and a certain depth with purple foliage. Pinks and mauves also work well with their complementary colors, lime or yellow-green.

PINK AND MAUVE vegetables

Cottager's kale		Its green leaves boast pale pink ribs. This is available in the United States but not in Europe, because of European Community regulations.
Ornamental cabbage	'Mizumi'	Cream, pink, and rose markings decorate its fluted leaves.
Runner bean	'Sunset'	Its pale pink flowers are followed by the first bean crop of the season.

PINK AND MAUVE herbs

Bergamot (*Monarda*)	'Croftway Pink'	This has pale pink flowers between June and August.
Chives		The small, tufted, green perennial makes a very good bed edging.

(continued on p. 168)

Stavordale Priory, Somerset, England

MR. AND MRS. LANGTON

In design and planting, the kitchen garden at Stavordale Priory is carried out almost entirely in cool-weather colors. This self-imposed discipline might have led to an effect of cool austerity, but the reverse is true. The beds have not been given clipped box or tile edgings, allowing the plantings to spill over and soften the lines of the pale-toned

Lupins provide accents of red and purple color, and they fix nitrogen in the soil.

paving. Depth of tone has been achieved through the use of dark green yews, both clipped and upright, which relieve the sometimes monotonous mid-green tones of vegetables. Finally, flower color softens the overall effect. The blues, mauves, and purples of campanulas, galegas, and columbines brighten the picture without compromising the overall "cool" color scheme. But the approach is not regimented. Where contrast is needed, clumps of orange-flowered calendulas complement the glaucous vegetable tones.

One of the Langtons' most important design decisions was to interpose an herb garden between their house and vegetable garden, so that evergreen herbs could provide a year-round foreground to the view from their windows. The length of the vegetable garden's lavender-lined walk is broken by a diamond of lavender in the center flanked by a pair of antique lead cisterns that serve a practical as well as a decorative function in the garden. Not only does their gray color echo that of the surrounding

Left: A lavender bed is set on a diagonal line to give visual movement to what might have been otherwise a static design. Note the well-crafted summer house and the unobtrusive fruit cage in the background.

Below: One of a pair of antique lead cisterns which serve an aesthetic as well as a practical function.

lavender, but the still water they hold at ambient temperature is much better for young seedlings than cold piped water from the mains.

The combination of ornament and utility is one of the keynotes of the garden. The fruit cage, necessary to protect ripening fruit from birds, is nevertheless carefully painted a matte black so that it does not attract the eye. Oriental poppies, grown for their mauve-to-purple flowers and silvery foliage that contribute to the color scheme, provide cans of seed for poppyseed cake. Lupins, cultivated for their blue and purple flower spikes, are useful as nitrogen-fixing legumes.

Another distinctive feature of the garden is the excellent craftsmanship displayed in its construction and cultivation. The wooden summer house, gates, and the low, stone boundary walls are all built in local, natural materials, to traditional specifications but without any architectural or stylistic pretensions. The bean tunnels and pea fences are so well crafted, using birch and hazel from a nearby wood, that they would not be out of place as sculptural installations in a contemporary art museum.

The detailed planning of the vegetable beds is traditional in approach. The perennial vegetables—rhubarb, asparagus, and artichoke—in the perimeter beds surround the annual vegetables in the center beds. All the plants are in rows rather than in the modern-format blocks. This means that the gardener must walk between the rows for access to the vegetables. The expected disadvantage of soil compaction is minimized at Stavordale, because the soil

is so open and airy. The excellent tilth of the soil also makes heavy labor and the use of large machinery unnecessary. Once the beds have been thoroughly dug and manured, they remain fertile for years.

No matter how well designed a garden is, it will look dull unless the details of its planting are constantly maintained. After a period of time, certain plants may be found to be unsatisfactory; the owner learns from such experiences and alters the planting accordingly. Happy accidents, such as a self-sown seedling whose flower brings drama to its neighbors, are remembered and repeated.

At Stavordale, there are many such unexpected combinations. The creamy plumes of goat's beard, *Aruncus sylvester*, light up the shadowy recesses under an Irish yew; pink-flowered *Rosa* 'Ballerina' was used as a standard rather than the ubiquitous *Rosa* 'Iceberg', and an unplanned diagonal path was introduced because of its success, but, as an extra surprise, its line was found to give movement to what would otherwise have been a very static design.

The Langtons' deliberate restraint in the design and planting of their garden creates an atmosphere of orderly calm. It is effective not only as an antidote to the stresses of modern life, but also as an appropriate setting for a house that began life as a medieval priory.

Purples and Reds

Red is the most commanding and eye-catching of all colors. It makes a bold visual exclamation mark when seen from afar. Nature uses it in moderation, usually in occasional spots of vivid color set against a wider background of low-toned gray or green foliage. As a highlight, it adds a note of warmth and sharp perspective to other tonal shades. Nature's model is a good one to follow when using red in the garden.

PURPLE AND RED vegetables

Broccoli	'Purple Sprouting'	This variety produces quantities of dark red–purple flower buds from February to April.
	'Rosalind'	A very cold-hardy variety with a large purple head that can be harvested in autumn or early winter.
Brussels sprouts	'Rubine'	A red-tinted sprout known to gourmets for its excellent flavor.
Cabbage	'Red Drumhead'	Its solid, round, dark-red, and fine-textured heads stand ready for harvesting over a long period.
	'Langedijker Early Norma'	Its smaller heads, which allow close planting, make the variety an ideal choice for a small garden.
Cauliflower	'Purple Cape'	A hardy variety with large purple curds instead of the usual white heads.
	'Violet Queen'	Its 8-inch-wide, deep-purple heads turn a rich green when boiled.
Chicory	'Alouette'	The upright leaves change with the onset of cold weather, from green to red. They also become more round and closely packed into a tight heart just above ground level.
Chinese cabbage	'Hen Tsai Tsai'	This flowering bok choy has deep purple ribs on its decorative green foliage.
French bean	'Purple Teepee'	This variety has dark purple pods that turn green when cooked.
Kale	'Ragged Jack'	An old-fashioned dwarf variety that has purple and blue-green serrated leaves.
Kohlrabi	'Purple Vienna'	Both the edible swollen stem and the mid-ribs of the green leaves are purple.
Leek	'Blue Solaise'	A variety with purple, swordlike leaves.
Lettuce	'May Queen'	A butterhead type with red-tinged leaves.
	'Trotzkoph'	Another butterhead type but with leaves that are variegated red and green.
	'Apache'	A cos type with outer leaves of a bronzy red and an inner heart of pink, cream, and green.

continues

Lettuce, *continued*	'Panella Red'	An iceberg type that is a red version of the hardy and compact green panella variety. It is also extremely decorative when allowed to bolt.
	'Rougette du Midi'	An iceberg type of a smaller size. It is also reddish-leaved and very decorative when allowed to bolt.
	'Lollo Rosso'	A variety characterized by its red-and-green variegated leaves that are frilled as well as crinkly.
	'Feuilles de Chene'	A variety with very indented, oak-leaved foliage.
Pea	'Purple-Podded'	This variety has ornamental purple pods containing nicely flavored green peas.
Perilla	'Red'	A bushy annual herb used in Japanese cooking. The color of the red-leaved forms ranges from pinkish and deep red to a rich bronze.
Red orach		A variety of the mountain spinach that is a tall (up to 6 feet) and decorative annual with red leaves.
Runner bean	'Caroby Maussance'	The flowers are a pale but attractive purple.
Rhubarb	'Hawke's Champagne'	This reliable early rhubarb has deep red stems.
Salsify	'Mammoth'	This biennial, with purple, daisylike flowers, is usually grown for its delicate-flavored roots. Its chards (young shoots), flower buds, and flowers can also be used to flavor salads.

PURPLE AND RED fruits

Apple	'Spartan'	A Canadian variety with very dark crimson, almost blackish fruit when ripe.
	'May Queen'	A small tree with heavy crops of fair-sized crimson apples.
Cherry	'Merton Glory'	Ideal for fan-training against a wall, it has large, heart-shaped fruit flushed with bright crimson.
Crab apple	'Dartmouth'	Like a small orchard apple, this variety has large, slender-stalked crimson fruit in October.
Greengage	'Count Althana's'	One of the most richly flavored greengages, the fruit is a dark crimson color speckled with golden dots.
Gooseberry	'May Duke'	This bush of upright growth carries large dark red fruit.
	'Whinhan's Industry'	A variety of spreading habit, carrying large, oval dark red berries.
Loganberry	'LT59'	The best loganberry with large maroon-colored fruit.
Plum	'Victoria'	The best-known plum with a prolific and regular crop of oval red plums.

PURPLE AND RED herbs

Purple basil	An annual whose leaves are widely used to flavor tomato salads.
Purple fennel	The dark purple-leaved form of this perennial. The seeds and young leaves are used to flavor fish and salads.
Purple sage	The purple-hued form of this most useful herb may be picked fresh all year-round.

Hot Colors

Hot colors evoke a mood of excitement. Their bright contrasts can be said to jolt the eye and disturb tranquillity, or to jar the mind from sleepy complacency. Hot colors tend to foreshorten perspective, especially in a small garden, where they can be too dominating, reducing the sense of space and inducing a sense of restlessness. If they are the principal color in the garden, the eye may tire too quickly. Their strident effect can be reduced by diluting them with "linked" cream, purple, or orange tones. On the other hand, the effect of hot colors will be exaggerated if they are used with silver or gray foliage. Hot colors are not always harsh: in a hot climate, they appear paler. And they can be used to enable objects that share their colors to retain their definition of form when seen from a distance.

HOT COLOR vegetables

Beetroot	'Bolthardy'	This variety, which has smooth-skinned roots of fine quality, is valuable for its resistance to bolting.
French bean	'Royal Standard'	Vigorous and cropping over a long period, this variety has bright red flowers before its pods are produced.
Pumpkin	'Jack Be Little'	The tiniest and most decorative pumpkin with bright orange, distinctly ribbed fruit.
	'Atlantic Giant'	This variety, by contrast, produces the largest fruit, popular for Halloween or Thanksgiving Day.
Ruby chard		Its green leaves have bright red mid-ribs, so scarlet that they clash with vegetables that are purple-red.
Runner bean	'Painted Lady'	The oldest known variety, it is sometimes called the York and Lancaster bean because of its scarlet and white flowers.
	'Hammond's Dwarf Scarlet'	A red-flowering dwarf form ideal for the small garden, it will crop for many weeks if picked regularly.

continues

Squash	'Red Kuri'	A variety with stunning bright orange, teardrop-shaped fruit.
	'Turk's Turban'	A decorative squash in the shape of a turban. Its basic color is bright orange-red with a prominent "button" marked with red, orange, green, and cream.
Sweet pepper	'Redskin'	As with many varieties, the fruit starts green but turns a rich, deep red as it matures.
	'Midnight Beauty'	The shining fruits of this variety begin purple and then turn deep red as they mature.
	'Long Yellow Ringo'	This variety produces long, sweet-flavored fruits, starting green but turning a rich yellow.
Tomato	'Gardener's Delight'	A tall-growing variety with bright red, thin-skinned fruit that requires cordon support.
	'Tiny Tim'	Bright red fruit is carried on this bush variety that does not need staking. As in many bush varieties, the fruit tends to be hidden by the foliage.

HOT COLOR fruits

Cherry	'Marchiana'	Like all varieties, best grown as a fan; this has orange-red berries.
Crab apple	'Veitch's Scarlet'	An outstanding crab whose white flowers are followed by conspicuous red fruits.
Red currant	'Red Lake'	A brightly colored fruit grown on the long branches of a bush with upright growth. It was recently introduced in the United States.
Strawberry	'Cambridge Favorite'	Its large dark fruit, with a pleasant pine flavor, are born in abundance in mid-season.

Opposite: Shocking colors add hints of dazzle in the kitchen garden.

FORM IN THE KITCHEN GARDEN

In recent years, much emphasis has been placed on flower color in the garden, often at the expense of other characteristics of plants, such as their foliage, fruit, stems, and overall form and texture. In fact, it is impossible to consider a plant's color without also thinking, even if only subconsciously, about its form and texture. The quality of light falling on a vegetable's foliage, for example, will depend on whether it is of upright or spreading habit, or whether its form is distinct or indistinct.

Solid Form

Plants whose leaves are set densely together have a solid outline or form. When plants like these are arranged in a group, each individual plant retains its own distinct shape. They do not "weave" together visually as do the individual forms of peas and beans. They can have a heavy and dull effect if their leaves are matte surfaced, or they can be bright and interesting if their leaves are glossy. The solid, globular

forms of 'Drumhead' cabbages can help create color contrasts that are dramatic but heavy. Their somewhat stiff habit can be counteracted by associating these solid plants with plants of softer, looser form. A bed of 'Drumhead' cabbage can be edged with lavender or interplanted with a catch crop of feathery carrot foliage. They can also be arranged to make patterns as precise as those in any formal parterre. Their strong forms can be balanced against wide backgrounds of looser, less distinct foliage. Their form can also be deliberately emphasized by placing them against a background of contrasting color tone, thus establishing a strong visual rhythm to link and unify an entire garden scheme.

Indistinct Forms

Plants of this classification have branches and leaves set well apart. The resulting open habit incorporates a good mixture of light and shade, giving a lightweight or airy appearance that is often enhanced by a breeze-driven shimmering movement of the leaves. Their insubstantial effect can be countered by associated plantings of a more formal nature; for example, a bed of peas or beans will be given substance and strength of form if sur-

Contrasting forms at Barnsley House—tight-clipped box, mounded brussels sprout foliage, and the open luxuriance of cabbage leaves.

rounded by a clipped box hedge or low mounds of more solid foliage. In making any plant associations of this kind, it is important to plan contrasts of height and of form. Too many plants of the same height in a bed give a two-dimensional effect that lacks the subtlety of cast shadows.

Architectural Forms

Plants of such strong and definite shape can often relegate neighboring plants to comparative unimportance. The taller kinds, like globe artichoke, are invaluable for their ability to visually link the other garden plants with the higher surrounding trees and hedges. Their symmetry of form results in their frequent use as sentinels to frame vistas or gateways.

WEEPING FORMS
vegetables

Yard-long bean	Sometimes called the asparagus bean. Like most so-called pendulous vegetables, this depends for its effect not on a weeping habit or on drooping foliage but on the clusters of extra-long hanging beans.

fruit

Prunus persica 'Windle Weeping'	A very distinct form of weeping peach with broad leaves and semidouble, cup-shaped flowers of purplish pink.

FASTIGIATE FORMS
vegetables

Lettuce	If uncropped lettuces are allowed to bolt, they will become tall cones that are admired in some gardens, such as Highgrove, for their sculptural shape.

fruits

Apples and pears	These can be grown as vertical cordons, i.e., pruned into an upright shape, making them ideal space-savers in a small garden.
Plums and greengages	These, as well as apples and pears, can be grown as dwarf pyramids by using dwarfing rootstock and pruning to a height of about 7 feet and a width of about 4 feet.

At Mudd's Restaurant in California: these rosettes of undulate leaves are characteristic of butterhead lettuce.

HORIZONTAL FORMS
vegetables

Nasturtium	Trailing nasturtiums, if planted closely together, will quickly form a ground carpet with a strong horizontal line.
Squash	Another vegetable with a trailing habit, squash offers the opportunity to create a strong horizontal line in the composition of the kitchen garden.

fruits

Alpine	Often used as a groundcover in a border or as an edging to a strawberry vegetable bed. The variegated form is attractive.
Apples	These can be trained along a low, horizontal wire stretched and pears between posts perhaps 18 inches above ground level to form a bed edging, or what is sometimes called a step-over fence.

GLOBOSE FORMS
vegetables

Chinese cabbage 'Pe-tsai'	It has either a cylindrical or a barrel-shaped head, depending on the variety.

fruits

Red and white currant	The aim in pruning is to achieve a goblet-shaped bush with an open center.
Gooseberry	This is ideally pruned into a broad globular shape, either as a bush or a standard.

Textural foliage contrasts in Nancy McCabe's garden in Connecticut.

TEXTURE IN THE KITCHEN GARDEN

The way in which light falls on a petal or leaf can dramatically alter its basic color. Depending on the amount of sunlight, the effect can be low-toned and mysterious on a leaf with a matte surface, or brilliant and exciting on one with a glossy surface. A smooth surface usually looks darker and purer in color than a matte or dull surface, on which roughness or hairs interfere with the direct reflection of light.

A kitchen garden, consisting mostly of low-toned foliage colors, relies, more than a flower garden, on the creative use of textures in its design. The filmy, "atmospheric" texture of asparagus foliage can be contrasted, for example, with the waxy, light-reflecting leaves of lettuce. The folded texture of brassica heads can be contrasted with the grassy foliage of onions. The angular, sculpted leaves of artichokes, the corrugated leaves of the Savoy cabbage, the curly tips of kale leaves, and the heavily serrated, indented edges of frisée lettuce leaves all provide opportunities for highlighting interesting visual effects. Large-leaved plants such as rhubarb and pumpkin can create an exotic, semitropical atmosphere, casting deep shadows and creating a feeling of space and distance. For maximum effect, use them as isolated elements against a wider background of foliage with a less distinct texture.

Large Leaves

Vegetables and fruit with large leaves usually need special attention—a cool, moist location, shelter from winds that may shred them, and protection from sun that may burn them.

LARGE LEAF vegetables

Rhubarb	Its large, jagged, reddish leaves can reach up to 18 inches in width. (Although they can be handled safely, the leaf blades are poisonous when eaten.)
Squash	Its large leaves are either lobed, round, or heart-shaped, depending on the variety.
Great burdock	Often growing to an impressive size, it has large, rough-textured leaves.
Sea kale	Clouds of tiny white flowers appear above the large, ice-blue leaves in early summer.

LARGE LEAF fruits

Kiwi	The climbing kiwi boasts large, heart-shaped leaves on densely hairy, reddish shoots.
Fig	The edible fig is a large shrub with handsome lobed leaves— an object of interest throughout the year.

Grassy Leaves

Plants that have small, narrow leaves and plumose flowers are often brought to life by breezes that cause them to wave and rustle. They also impart a lightness to the scene that no other plants can give.

GRASSY LEAF vegetables

Corn	Corns are tall, annual grasses. Ornamental corns come in a marvelous array of colors, shapes, and sizes but are not as palatable as sweet corn.
Chives	These form dense, mounding clumps of fine, gray-green leaves.
Lemon grass	A tropical perennial grown as an annual in cooler climates. It forms clumps of coarse, sharp-edged, grasslike leaves.

Sword Leaves

Usually growing in clusters and with a strength of line provided by no other plants, they are a strong focus for the eye and a good contrast for plants of rounded or open-growing habit.

SWORD LEAF vegetables

Onions	These are half-hardy perennials grown as long-season annuals. Each sheaf of leaves is often bent over to speed ripening in late August or September.
Garlic	A perennial, its large flattened leaves are somewhat like those of bearded iris.
Leeks	This hardy winter vegetable has a stemlike collection of large, flattened leaves.

Feathery Leaves

Plants with tall, delicate sprays of minute leaves and graceful growth act as a foil for plants of more decisive outline.

FEATHERY LEAF vegetables

Florence fennel	Its finely divided, needlelike foliage resembles that of dill but is apple-green instead of bluish-green.
Dill	Its blue-green, lacy foliage is topped with umbrellalike clusters of yellow flowers.
Sweet cicely	Its fernlike leaves and clusters of white flowers give to this plant a delicacy of character hardly matched in any other kitchen garden plant.
Asparagus	Feathery foliage decorates the spears that have been left unharvested.

Rough-Textured Leaves

Rough texture in foliage usually occurs when the leaf venation is sunk deep and the fleshy part of the leaf between the veins rises in irregular forms.

ROUGH-TEXTURED LEAF vegetables

Swiss chard	Its triangular leaves are spectacularly ridged.
Cabbage 'Savoy King'	It has distinctly crinkly leaves as have many of the ornamental cabbages. (Only the center or young leaves of the latter varieties are palatable.)
Curled kale	Its erect green to deep blue-green leaves have fringed or wavy edges. (The more decorative ornamental kales are edible, but are not bred to be palatable.)
Curly endive	Its leaves are curled and deeply cut.

ROUGH-TEXTURED LEAF fruit

Raspberry	Its densely corrugated leaves have pronounced serrations.

Smooth-Textured Leaves

Plants with smooth, glossy foliage appear to spring forward. When composing a view in the garden, an illusion of greater space can be created by placing plants with light-reflecting leaves in the foreground and those with matte leaves in the background.

SMOOTH-TEXTURED LEAF vegetables

Radicchio	These leaf chicory varieties, with tight heads in a deep green or magenta color, boast very shiny leaves.
Butterhead lettuce	The small, loosely folded head and the rosettes of ground-hugging leaves of the butterhead lettuces glisten.
Bay	Its dark, glossy, evergreen leaves are often clipped to make a formal shape in a kitchen garden.

SMOOTH-TEXTURED LEAF fruits

Peach	'Peregrine' Usually fan-trained against a wall, this peach has glistening, pointed leaves.
Pear	Pears have oval or rounded, glossy green leaves, depending on the variety.

Soft-Textured Leaves

The use of plants with quiet, matte-textured leaves helps a garden merge visually into its surroundings. Their visually recessive quality can be used to make a small garden look bigger while adding a sense of warmth to the garden.

SOFT-TEXTURED LEAF vegetables

Eggplant	It makes an upright bush with large softly furry leaves growing on stiff shoots.
Perilla	This tall, half-hardy annual is grown for its furry, but edible, green or purple leaves.
Pelargonium	Some varieties have soft leaves that can be used fresh in baking, to flavor fruit cups, or in beverages.

SOFT-TEXTURED LEAF fruit

Vitis vinifera 'Dusty Miller'	This grapevine has gray-green leaves with a white, cobwebby down.

Conclusion

There never has been a better time to start a kitchen garden. The fitness enthusiast, the health food zealot, the cost-conscious consumer, and, above all, the gourmet can testify to the unique advantage of eating home-grown food. The fitness enthusiast is aware that gardening is one of the most mentally and physically satisfying activities there is. There is a sheer sensual pleasure from producing fresh, beautiful fruit and vegetables, and there is a mental relaxation that is the result of performing the many routine tasks associated with gardening. The production of food is one of the most primitive, yet now sadly neglected, of human activities. The value of the physical exercise, which involves almost the whole range of human musculature, is testified to by gardeners' traditional longevity. Hugh Johnson, the

well-known writer on wine and trees, affirms, "A well-done kitchen garden is more expressive of the harmony of man and nature than anything else a gardener can do." In summary, a kitchen garden is not just a plot full of useful plants, but a symbol of a wider vision of nature that succors both body and spirit.

The health food zealot is acutely aware of the joys of eating fresh garden produce untainted by inorganic fertilizers, weedkillers, pesticides, or the sprays often used to keep commercial produce fresh before it arrives on the supermarket shelf. Not only does a small-scale kitchen garden produce fruit and vegetables that are more robust, that stay fresh longer, and that are richer in vitamin C than their store-bought equivalents, but they are a most environmentally friendly way of cultivating and sustaining the land. The cost-conscious consumer will concentrate on growing the rarer and more expensive crops, such as asparagus, so that their labor will have its rewards in lower-priced foods.

The gourmet, however, is the most obvious beneficiary of a home-based kitchen garden, enjoying the tastes of the widest possible range of:

Young Fruit and Vegetables: Compare the mild flavor of a baby leek, carrot, or turnip, with the coarse, slightly abrasive taste of the larger, more mature vegetable; or the smallest spinach leaves so tender they can be eaten in a green salad, with the mature foliage that needs to be cooked to make it palatable.

Fruit and Vegetables at Their Peak: Compare peak produce with store-bought produce that is cropped to suit the storage and shipping schedules of the large commercial grower. Consider, for example, the zucchini, which is best eaten together with its flower. For one day in the life of the female zucchini, its bloom is at its peak, and this is the day the vegetable should be picked. Cutting zucchinis in flower is a delicate operation—the petals of the tender yellow blooms are easily torn on the sharp edge of a leaf or on the prickly stem of the main flower. The possibility of producing vegetables in such a state of perfection for the kitchen is the prerogative of the home grower.

Fresh Fruit and Vegetables: Freshly picked, sun-warmed fruit is far superior to store-bought produce, because its subtle flavors and textures can be marred by mechanical handling or wrapping. Particularly striking is the difference between the distinct, tart taste and firm texture of fresh red or white currants and those that have often disintegrated to pulp by the time they are bought by the consumer from the supermarket shelf. Similarly, salad crops and vegetables such as peas, carrots, asparagus, tomatoes, and sweet corn give a totally new flavor experience if served within an hour or two of harvesting. They need only a minimum of "culinary" treatment—just enough to enhance, but never to disguise or conceal, the natural flavor. Lightly cooked borscht, the beetroot soup of central Europe, is incomparable when made within minutes of picking the vegetable. Preserves and jams made

with fresh produce also provide a delightful change from the bland and predictable flavors of their commercial counterparts.

Uncommon Fruit and Vegetable Varieties: There are between 100 and 150 different salad plants, yet how many do we ever see in shops?

Many vegetables like kohlrabi, celeriac, sweet pepper, or the Chinese and Japanese vegetables whose seed is now available in ethnic or "alternative" seed shops, are rarely if ever seen on the shelf. The many unusual strains of common vegetables are also interesting to

try. These can be either historical varieties or geographical varieties. Many old fruit and vegetable varieties with wonderful flavor, such as the potatoes 'Epicure' and 'King Edward', are no longer grown because they are low yielding or disease prone. The European Union has forbidden the cultivation and marketing of many of them. However, those interested can obtain banned varieties from the Henry Doubleday Research Association (see list of sources on page 188) through a special arrangement, especially if you are prepared to become a "seed guardian." Seed guardians volunteer to raise rare vegetable varieties and agree to let some of the crop run to seed. The seed is collected and returned to the seed bank maintained by the HDRA as part of their conservation program. Private gardeners may take part in the scheme, which demands a methodical approach and a certain degree of horticultural skill, especially with vegetables that are apt to cross-pollinate. Geographical varieties of common vegetables result from different regions growing their own traditional strains over long periods of time. The white-flowered kale, which for centuries has been the staple diet of northern Portugal, appears as a yellow-flowered form in neighboring Spain. Joy Larkcom reported collecting seed of over 100 such regional varieties on her year's journey through Europe in

search of unusual vegetables and growing techniques. The traveling kitchen gardener can search out such varieties in local flower markets or seed shops, bring them home to grow, and enjoy their distinct flavors.

Unusual Parts of Common Vegetables: The store-buyer will be able to taste only the root of a beetroot, but never its tender young leaves. The turnip has delicately flavored young stalks, and snap peas have delicious white flowers and curling tendrils. The kitchen gardener will be able to enjoy eating the flowers of French beans, peas, radish, salsify, scorzonera, and radicchio, but only the main part of the vegetable is for sale in the grocery store.

Edible Flowers: There are few pleasures that match devouring the flowers of marigolds, sage, nasturtium, chrysanthemum, gladiolus, rosemary, mallow, and

primrose. Heartsease pansies are also reserved for those who grow their own, as a florist's may not be free from harmful sprays.

An integral part of the gourmet's satisfaction in owning a vegetable plot is the opportunity to take guests on a leisurely, after-dinner stroll to inspect the garden from whence the recently consumed fresh produce came. This was a common diversion in nineteenth-century England.

Not only have the advantages of fresh garden produce become apparent during the last few years, but the technique of kitchen gardening has never been easier. Its quick results suit the temperament and social mobility of the present age. Most foods are annual crops. Radishes, for example, take only 3 weeks from sowing to harvesting; lettuces only 50

days; tomatoes no more than 3 months. A one-season endeavor, it also satisfies the beginner's desire for rapid results. Worldwide research is also producing hardier and more reliable fruit and vegetables that mature faster, yield more, crop more easily, are more disease resistant, and are free of viruses.

British plant breeders have developed new brussels sprouts, cabbages, cauliflowers, carrots, peas, and potatoes. Dutch breeders have been working on improving onions, leeks, and lettuce, and the Japanese have made some significant contributions to cabbage, calabrese, and over-wintering onions. The United States is a source of new varieties of peas, dwarf French beans, and sweet corn. Australia and Denmark have provided new strains of autumn cauliflower and soft fruit such as loganberries. The most

significant development, however, is the breeding of new dwarf varieties of plants like French beans that do not need staking and tying, blackberries and raspberries with very short canes, and apples and pears that are bushes rather than trees. All of these new developments make it possible to now have a complete kitchen garden on a small plot.

For over a century, city dwellers in countries like England, Poland, and Russia have been able to have individual kitchen gardens on what are called allotments, pieces of common land set aside and divided up by municipalities for that purpose. The average size of an allotment was based on the amount of ground required to keep a family of four in fruit and vegetables the year-round. This was usually assessed as being about 100 feet by 30 feet, with an addition-

al 30 feet by 30 feet if main crop potatoes were to be grown as well. With present day techniques of close-planting and deep cultivation, combined with the increased availability of dwarf plant varieties, a plot of much smaller size—just 30 feet by 30 feet—is sufficient to keep the same family of four in lettuces, peas, summer beans, carrots, and turnips during the summer, with leeks, cabbages, and sprouts in the winter. A smaller plot, 10 feet by 30 feet, will grow salads, tomatoes, beans, onions, and perhaps fruit and other crops for a family of four. Those with an even smaller plot, half that size, for example, need not despair. It will be sufficient to keep the same family in salads and tomatoes for much of the year. (People often ask how much time the maintenance of a kitchen garden absorbs—the answer is, one hour a day or its equivalent per week for a family kitchen garden in full production.)

Town house and apartment dwellers can also participate in kitchen gardening. On a paved patio, runner beans can be trained up tepees in tubs, and strawberries can be grown in large strawberry pots. Lettuces, salad onions, tomatoes, and cucumbers can be grown in raised beds, and cordon gooseberries, red currents, and vines, against a wall. *New York Times* gardening writer Linda Yang has described her blueberry garden on the roof terrace of her nineteenth floor mid-town Manhattan apartment and the ecstasy on her children's faces as they bring in bowls of blueberries for breakfast in September. Apartment-dwellers can garden on balconies or in window boxes. The choices of high-rise apartment owners will be restricted by windy conditions and sometimes scorching summer heat prevailing on their balconies, but quick salad crops and runner beans will thrive in decorative tubs and boxes. High-

rise apartments in Moscow and Leningrad are shaded in summer by runner beans growing on strings stretched from window boxes to lintels. Anyone who lives in a low-level apartment can grow herbs and salads in window boxes, and dwarf tomatoes in hanging baskets. Even those without exterior space can participate in the new kitchen gardening movement, as a sunny kitchen will give enough light for tomatoes, mustard, cress, and chives to be grown inside, and a darker spot will provide fertile ground for a mushroom crop.

The culinary benefits of a kitchen garden are unquestionable, but can it look decorative? Is it conceivable that it might replace the conventional lawn and shrub borders that surround most houses of an average size today? Too often, vegetables have been banished to a distant patch behind a screen, while the fruit garden with its frames, cages, and wired or netted enclosures resembles a zoo. However, the decorative qualities of fruit and vegetables have long been appreciated by the Dutch still-life painters. Artists such as Arcimboldo and sculptors like Grinling Gibbons have espoused the beauty of vegetable gardens. In the eighteenth century, Thomas Addison proclaimed himself "more pleased to survey my rows of colworts and cabbage, with a thousand nameless pot-herbs springing up in their full fragrance and verdure, than to see the tender plants of foreign countries." When runner beans, tomatoes, and asparagus were first introduced into Europe, they were cultivated as ornamental rather than food plants, as it was thought they rivaled conventional plants in the beauty of their flower and foliage. Vegetables like fennel and globe artichokes have long been judged sufficiently

decorative to be included in the planting of conventional flower borders. Beetroot, Swiss chard, carrots, and dwarf lettuces have often been grown as attractive groundcovers. Chives, thyme, parsley, asparagus, and peas make good border edgings and many vegetables, such as yellow-flowered scorzonera, make wonderful splashes of floral color in season. What could be prettier than a 'Salad Bowl' lettuce, a 'Brant' grapevine on a wall, a bank of wild strawberries, or an apple tree such as 'Ribston Pippin' with its handsome fruit and its dark leaves with pale undersides? Even rows of onions ripening in the late summer or cockades of winter-standing leeks can be attractive if fitted into an overall decorative design. Combining vegetables in an informal

arrangement like that of a flower border was Gertrude Jekyll's idea. She wrote in her understated way, "I have often thought what a beautiful bit of summer gardening one could do, merely planting with things usually grown in the kitchen garden only."

The aim of this book has been to show that the kitchen garden can not only provide a taste experience for a new generation and revitalize the distant memories of fresh produce among older people, it can not only give us back the sharpness of taste and smell that existed before the gradual deterioration of our senses through the eating of shop-bought produce, but it can also be as refined a place as any flower or shrub garden, as much by its overall design as by its meticulous execution and judicious choice of plants.

Resources

Suppliers of Seeds and Plants

SELECT LIST OF U.S. VEGETABLE SEED SUPPLIERS

General

W. Atlee Burpee & Co
Warminster, Pennsylvania 18974

The Cook's Garden
Box 535
Londonderry, Vermont 05148

Earl May Seed & Nursery Co.
Shenandoah, Iowa 51603

Johnny's Selected Seeds
310 Foss Hill Road
Albion, Maine 04910

J.W. Jung Seed Co.
Randolph, Wisconsin 53957

Park Seed Co.
Cokesbury Road
Greenwood, South Carolina 29648

Shepherd's Garden Seeds
30 Irene Street
Torrington, Connecticut 06790

Stark Bro.'s Nurseries
Louisiana, Missouri 63353

Stokes Seeds Inc.
1516 Stokes Building
Buffalo, New York 14240

Thompson & Morgan Inc.
P.O. Box 1308
Jackson, New Jersey 08527

Vermont Bean Seed Company
Garden Lane
Fair Haven, Vermont 05743

Specialist

Epicure Seeds Ltd.
Avon, New York 14414

Kitzawa Seed Co.
356 W. Taylor Street
San Jose, California 95110

Seed Savers Exchange
Kent Whealy, RR 2
Princeton, Montana 64673

SELECT LIST OF U.K. VEGETABLE SEED SUPPLIERS

General

J.W. Boyce
Bush Pasture
Lower Carton Street, Fordham
Nr. Ely, Cambridge CB7 5JU

Samuel Dobie and Sons, Ltd.
Broomhill Way
Torquay, Devon TQ2 7QW

Suttons Seeds, Ltd.
Hele Road
Torquay, Devon TQ2 7QJ

Thompson & Morgan
London Road
Ipswich, Suffolk 1P2 0BA

Unwins Seeds, Ltd.
Histon, Cambridge CB4 473

Specialist

John Chambers
15 Westleigh
Barton Seagrave
Kettering, Northants NN15 5AJ
(edible wild plants and unusual edible plants)

Chiltern Seeds
Bortree Stile
Ulverston, Cumbria LA12 7PB
(Oriental and unusual vegetables)

Henry Doubleday Research Association (HDRA)
Centre for Organic Gardening
Ryton-on-Dunsmore, Coventry CV8 3LQ
(old and rare varieties)

Mr. Fothergill's Seeds
Gazely Road
Kentford
Newmarket, Suffolk CB8 7QB
(unusual varieties of vegetables)

W. Robinson & Sons, Ltd.
Sunny Bank
Forton
Nr. Preston, Lancs PR3 0BN
(mammoth range of vegetables)

Suffolk Herbs
Sawyers Farm
Little Cornald
Sudbury, Suffolk CO10 0PF
(Oriental vegetables)

SELECT LIST OF U.S. FRUIT NURSERYMEN

General

Burnt Ridge Nursery
432 Burnt Ridge Road
Onalaska, Washington 98570

Edible Landscaping
Box 77
Afton, Virginia 22920

Plumtree Nursery
387 Springtown Road
New Paltz, New York 12561

Raintree Nursery and Northwood Nursery
391 Butts Road
Morton, Washington 98356

Southmeadow Fruit Gardens
Lakeside, Michigan 49116

Tolowa Nursery
360 Stephen Way
Williams, Oregon 92010

Specialist

J.E. Miller Nurseries
Canandaigua, New York 14424

Pacific Tree Farms
4301 Lynwood Drive
Chula Vista, California 92010

Pinetree Garden Seeds
New Gloucester, Maine 04260

Rare Fruit Nursery
1065 Messenger Road
Grant's Pass, Oregon 97527

Sherwin Akins Greenhouses
P.O. Box 6
Sibley, Louisiana 71073

SELECT LIST OF U.K. FRUIT NURSERYMEN

General

James Coles & Sons Ltd.
The Nurseries
Thurnby, Leics LE7 9QB

Deacons Nursery
Godshill, Isle of Wight PO38 3HW

Highfield Nurseries
Whitminster, Gloucester GL2 7PL

Keepers Nursery
446 Wateringbury Road
East Malling
Maidstone, Kent ME199 6JJ

Frank P. Matthews, Ltd.
Berrington Court
Tenbury Wells, Worcestershire WR15 8TH

New Trees Nurseries
22 Nunnery Road
Canterbury, Kent CT1 3LF

Sherrards
The Garden Centre
Wantage Road
Donnington
Newbury, Berks RG16 9BE

Scotts Nurseries (Merriott) Ltd.
Merriott, Somerset TA16 5PL
(most comprehensive range of fruit)

J. Tweedie Fruit Trees
504 Denby Dale Road West
Calder Grove
Wakefield, Yorks WF4 3DB

Specialist

Ballerina Trees, Ltd.
Maris Lane
Trumpington, Cambridge C32 2LQ (columnar
apple trees)

Eden Nurseries
Rectory Land
Old Bolingbroke
Spilsby, Lines PE23 4EY
(hardy varieties of English apple trees)

Family Trees
Summerlands
Curdridge Botley, Hampshire SO3 2EA
(field-grown unusual fruit)

Kingsley Strawberries, Ltd.
Headley Mill Farm
Bordon, Hants GU35 8RH
(extensive range of strawberries—many varieties
grown under licence)

Ken Muir
Honeypot Farm
Rectory Road
Weeley Heath, Essex CO16 9BJ
(cane and bush fruit)

Read's Nursery
Hales Hall
Loddon, Norfolk NR14 6QW
(tender and/or greenhouse fruit)

T.A. Redman, Ltd.
Elms Farm
Ancton Lane
Middleton-on-Sea
Bognor Regis, West Sussex PO22 6N5
(bush and fan trained fruit)

Roughman Hall Nurseries (RHN Ltd)
Ipswich Road
Rougham
Bury St. Edmunds, Suffolk IP30 9LZ
(gooseberries)

Kitchen Gardens
Open to the Public

THE UNITED STATES

Atlanta Botanical Garden, Georgia
1345 Piedmont Avenue
Atlanta, Georgia 30309
Tel: (404) 876-5859

Atlanta Historical Society, Georgia
130 West Taces Ferry Road Northwest
Atlanta, Georgia 30305
Tel: (404) 814-4000

Barret House, New Hampshire
Main Street
New Ipswich, New Hampshire 03071
Tel: (603) 878-2517

Dow Garden, Michigan
1018 West Main Street
Midland, Michigan 48640
Tel: (517) 631-2677

Israel Crane House Gardens, New Jersey
110 Orange Road
Montclair, New Jersey 07042
Tel: (201) 744-1796

Monticello, Virginia
VA Rte. 53
Charlottesville, Virginia 22902
Tel: (804) 984-9822

Mount Vernon, Virginia
Mount Vernon Memorial Parkway
Mount Vernon, Virginia 22121
Tel: (703) 780-2000

Old Economy Village and Gardens, Pennsylvania
14th and Church Streets
Ambridge, Pennsylvania 15003
Tel: (412) 266-4500

Pennsbury Manor, Pennsylvania
400 Pennsbury Memorial Road
(off Bordontown Road, near Tullytown)
Morrisville, Pennsylvania 19067
Tel: (215) 946-0400

Putnam Cottage, Connecticut
243 Putnam Avenue
Greenwich, Connecticut 06830
Tel: (203) 869-9697

Sandoz Fruit Farm, Nebraska
HC 65, Box 42
Rushville, Nebraska
Tel: (308) 327-2560

Thornton House, Georgia
P.O. Box 778
Stone Mountain Park
Stone Mountain, Georgia 30086

Wyck, Pennsylvania
6026 Germantown Avenue
Philadelphia, Pennsylvania 19123
Tel: (215) 848-1690

BELGIUM
Chateau de Hex (Comtesse D'Ursel)
Hex, nr. Tongeren, B-3870 Hex.
Tel: 012 744 615
Open by appointment
(a vegetable garden remodeled from the original in
the early 1900s)

CANADA
Les Quatre Vents (Francis F. Cabot)
La Malbaie, Quebec G5A 1A2
Tel: (418) 434-2209
Open 4 or 5 days a week from May to August
Reservations: Centre Ecologique de Pont au Saumon
(potager of contemporary design)

FRANCE
Abbaye de Fontevraud (The State)
Fontevraud, nr. Saumur 49590
Tel: 41 51 7141
Open
(recently completed medieval garden, with vegetable
garden and orchard)

Jardin de Miromesnil (M. de Vogue)
Offranville, Normandy
Tel: 35 85 0280
Open
(large traditional potager)

Jardin Kahn, Musée Albert Kahn
(Departement des Hauts-de-Seine)
Rue des Abondances
Boulogne-Billancourt, Paris
Tel: 14 60 45280
Open
(ornamental fruit garden)

Le Manoir de Criqueboeuf (M. Y. Brynner)
Bonnebosq, Normandy
Open to specialists by written appointment only
(large contemporary potager)

Parc Balbi
(Ecole Nationale Supérieure d'Horticulture)
Rue su maréchal Joffre, Versailles
Tel: 39 50 6087 or 39 02 7103
Open
(the former *potage du roi,* the Royal Kitchen Garden
of Louis XIV)

Parc du Château de Villandry
(M. and Mme. R. Carvallo)
Soué-los-Tour-Villandry, The Loire
Tel: 47 50 0209
Open
(ornamental potager)

Saint-Jean-de-Beauregard
(M. and Mme. Bernard de Curel)
91940 Saint-Jean-de-Beauregard, nr. Paris
Tel: 60 12 0001
Open (old potager, being restored)

IRELAND

Kinoith (Darina Allen)
Shanagarry, Co. Cork
Tel: (021) 646 785
Open
(large modern kitchen garden, attached to
cooking school)

THE NETHERLANDS

Menkenmaborg
(Stiching Groningen Museum voor Stad en Lande)
Menkanawg 2
Uithuizen 9981 CV
Tel: (59) 543 1970
Open
(kitchen garden planted with soft fruit and
vegetables, also a *berceau* of pear trees and an
apple orchard)

THE UNITED KINGDOM

Barnsley House (Mrs. Rosemary Verey)
Barnsley, nr. Cirencester, Glos. GL7 5E
Tel: (0285) 740281
Open
(formal modern garden potager)

Barrington Court (The National Trust)
Nr. Ilminster, Somerset TA19 0NQ
Tel: (0460) 241 480
Open
(large walled kitchen garden, with excellent displays
of fruit and vegetables)

Berrington Hall (The National Trust)
Nr. Leominster, Herefordshire HR6 0DW
Tel: (0568) 615 721
Open
(local apple collection)

Calke Abbey (The National Trust)
Ticknall, Derbyshire DE73 1LE
Tel: (0332) 863822
Open
(kitchen garden being restored)

Felbrigg Hall (The National Trust)
Nr. Norwich, Norfolk NR11 8PR
Tel: (026) 387 444
Open
(large walled garden, with small orchard and fruit
and vegetable garden)

Hillbarn House (Mr. and Mrs. A. J. Buchanan)
Great Bedwyn, Nr. Hungerford, Wilts
Open 2 days a year (see National Gardens Scheme
booklet for dates)
(mixed potager and flower garden)

Quarry Bank Mill (The National Trust)
Apprentice House Garden
Styal, Wilmslow
Cheshire SK9 4LA
Tel: (0625) 527468
Open
(Victorian fruit and vegetable kitchen garden)

The Old Rectory, Sudborough
(Mr. and Mrs. Huntington)
Nr. Brigstock, Northants
Open
(formal, modern jardin potager)

Upton House (The National Trust)
Banbury, Oxfordshire I56 HT
Tel: (029) 567 0266
Open
(large impressive kitchen garden)

Suggested Reading

Arkin, Frieda. *The Essential Kitchen Gardener.* New York: Henry Holt and Co., 1989.

Baker, Harry. "Fruit." In *The RHS's Encylopaedia of Practical Gardening.* London: Mitchell Beazley, 1980.

Bicknell, Andres. *The New Kitchen Garden.* London: Viking, 1990.

Biachini, Francesco, Francesco Corbella, and Marilena Pistoia. *Fruits of the Earth.* London: Cassell, 1973.

Biggs, Tony. "Vegetables." In *The RHS's Encyclopaedia of Practical Gardening.* London: Mitchell Beazley, 1980.

Brookes, John. *Improve Your Lot.* London: Heinemann, 1977.

———. "Vegetables," "Fruit," "The Beauty of the Kitchen Garden," "Decorative Vegetables," and "Garden Fruit." In *The Small Garden.* London: Marshall Cavendish, 1977.

Chowings, J. W., and M. J. Day. *Vegetable Varieties for the Gardener.* London: Royal Horticultural Society, 1990.

Church, Thomas D. *Gardens Are for People.* New York: Rheinhold, 1955.

Clarke, Ethne. *The Art of the Kitchen Garden.* London: Michael Joseph, 1988.

Creasey, Rosalind. *Cooking from the Garden.* San Francisco: Sierra Club Books, 1988.

Crocket, James Underwood. *Vegetables and Fruits.* Amsterdam: Time-Life Books, 1972.

Dargan, Mary Palmer. *The Early English Kitchen Garden.* Charleston, South Carolina: Garden History Association, 1984.

Davies, Jennifer. *The Victorian Kitchen Garden.* London: BBC Books, 1987.

Douglas, William Lake, Susan K. Frey, Norman K. Johnston, Susan Littlefield, and Michael van Valkenburgh. "Edible Horticulture." In *Garden Design*. New York, London: Simon & Schuster, 1984.

Forsell, Mary. *Berries*. New York: Bantam, 1989.

———. *Heirloom Herbs*. New York: Villard, 1990.

Greenoak, Francesa. *Fruit and Vegetable Gardens*. London: Pavilion, 1990. In *The National Trust Guide to the Productive Garden*. Penelope Hobhouse, series ed.

Harvey, John. "Vegetables in the Middle Ages." In *Garden History*, vol. 12, no. 2. London: The Journal of the Garden History Society, Autumn 1984.

Harrison, S. G., G. B. Masefield, and Michael Wallis. *The Oxford Book of Food Plants*. Oxford: Oxford University Press, 1969.

Hatch, Peter J. *The Gardens of Monticello*. Charlottesville, Virginia: The Thomas Jefferson Memorial Foundation (n.d.).

Hessayon, D. G. *The Vegetable Expert*. Waltham Cross, England: PBI Publications, 1985.

Hobhouse, Penelope. *Colour in Your Garden*. London: Collins, 1985.

Holt, Geraldene. *The Gourmet Garden*. London: Pavilion, 1990.

Jellicoe, Geoffrey, Susan Jellicoe, Patrick Goode, and Michael Lancaster. "Kitchen Garden." In *The Oxford Companion to Gardens*. Oxford: Oxford University Press, 1985.

Johnson, Hugh. "The Kitchen Garden: The Principles." In *The Principles of Gardening*. London: Mitchell Beazley, 1979.

Jones, Louisa. *The Art of French Vegetable Gardening*. New York: Artisan, 1995.

Kellam de Forest, Elizabeth. *The Gardens and Grounds at Mount Vernon*. Mount Vernon, Virginia: The Mount Vernon Ladies Association of the Union, 1982.

Kourik, Robert. *Designing and Maintaining Your Edible Landscape Naturally*. Emmaus, Pennsylvania: Rodale Press, 1986.

Larkcom, Joy. *Vegetables from Small Gardens*. London: Faber & Faber, 1976.

———. *The Salad Garden*. London: Frances Lincoln/Windward, 1984.

———. "Oriental Vegetables." In *The Complete Guide for Garden and Kitchen*. London: John Murray, 1991.

Littlefield, Susan. "The Kitchen Garden." In *Visions of Paradise*. New York: Stewart, Tabori and Chang, 1985.

Nichols, Frederick D., and James A. Bear, Jr. *Monticello—A Guide Book.* Charlottesville, Virginia: The Thomas Jefferson Memorial Foundation, 1982.

Ogden, Shep, and Ellen Ogden. *The Cook's Garden.* Emmaus, Pennsylvania: Rodale Press, 1989.

Raphael, Sandra, ed. *An Oak Spring Pomona.* Virginia: The Oak Spring Garden Library, 1990.

Reader's Digest Association, eds. *Food from Your Garden.* New York: The Reader's Digest Association, 1987.

Reich, Lee. *Uncommon Fruits Worthy of Cultivation.* Reading, Massachusetts: Addison-Wesley, 1991.

"The Return of the Kitchen Garden." *Garden Design,* Special Issue, Summer 1990.

Seddon, George, and Helena Radecka. *Your Kitchen Garden.* London: Mitchell Beazley, 1975.

Shepherd, Renee. *Recipes from a Kitchen Garden.* Torrington, Connecticut: Shepherd Publishing, 1989.

Spoczynska, Joy O. I. *The Indoor Vegetable Garden.* North Pomfret, Vermont and Newton Abbot, England: David & Charles, 1986.

Swain, Roger B. *The Practical Gardener.* New York: Henry Holt and Co., 1989.

Toyne, David. *Vegetable Gardening.* London: Hamlyn, 1989.

Verey, Rosemary. *Classic Garden Design.* London: John Murray, 1984.

de Wolf, Gordon P., Jr., and others. *Taylor's Guide to Vegetables and Herbs.* Boston: Houghton, Mifflin, 1987.

Note: In *The Garden*, published by The Journal of The Royal Horticultural Society, there are numerous articles on kitchen gardens and on their fruits, nuts and vegetables.

Zone Map

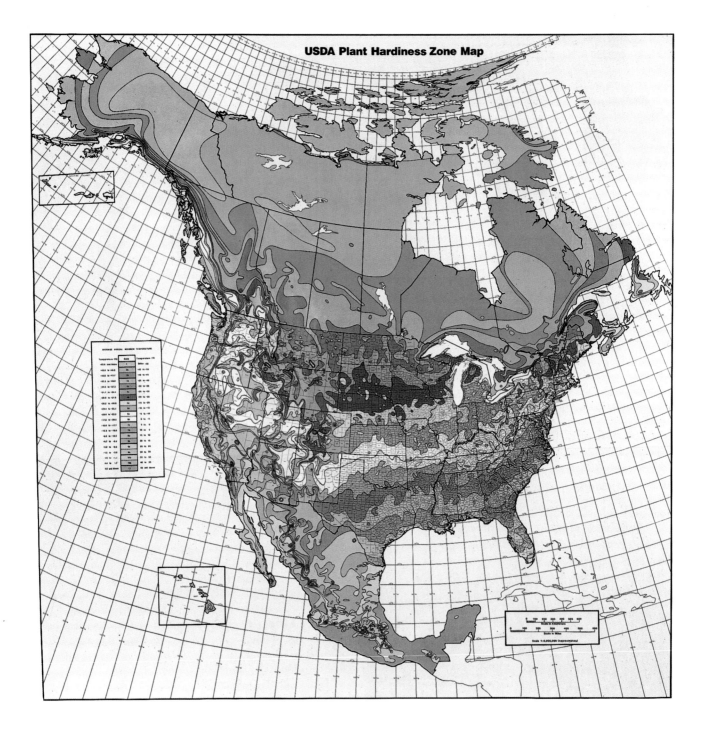

Index

Page numbers in *italic* refer to illustrations.

A

Abbadia a Coltibuono, 78
Actinidia chinensis, 86
Addison, Thomas, 186
Aix-en-Provence, 63
Allotments, 185
Alpine strawberries, 10, 49, 160, 176
Androuet du Cerceau, Jacques, 34
Antique garden ornaments, 101, 102, 104, 166–67
Apartments, 185–86
Apples
  as bed edging, 176
  cordons, 175
  dwarf, 53
  espaliers, 53
  'May Queen,' 169
  protecting from wasps, 12
  'Spartan,' 169
  training, 7–9, *7, 18*
  tunnels, 77, 79–82
The Apprentice House, 128
Apricots, 53
  'Moor Park,' 160
Arbors, 7, 69–72, *80, 82*
  iron, 70, 71–72
  trelliswork, 70, 71
Arches, 69–70, *71,* 72
  pears, 72, 74
  quince, 73–74, *73*

Art
  garden design ideas from, 34–35
  Islamic, 35, *35, 36*
  modern, 35
Artichokes, *155*
  globe, 32, 33, 186
  'Gros Vert de Leon,' 157
  Jerusalem, 33, 67
The Art of Gardening
  (Worlidge), 34, *34*
Asarina scandens, 72
Asparagus, 33, 178, 186
Atlanta (Georgia), gardens in, *31, 101, 143*
Avignon, 63

B

Bagneux, M. and Mme.
  Adalbert de, garden of, *25,* 123, 129–32, *129, 130–31, 132*
Bales, Suzanne F., *64*
Bamboo fences, 64
Barnsley House, 4–12, *7, 9, 10*
  beds, *4, 122,* 123, *123,* 128, *128,* 136, *139, 174*
  brick paths, *5,* 6–7, *6, 40*
  cabbages, 142
  colors, *148, 149,* 156

plans, *8, 11,* 34, 156
undercropping, *137*
vegetable tunnels, *6, 7,* 72, *77*
Basil, purple, 171
Bay, 179
Beans
  broad, 157
  fences, *114*
  French, 82, 85, *158,* 159, 168, 171
  lablab, *6, 7*
  runner, 7, 32, 72, 85, 114, 157, 164, 169, 171, 186
  tents, *107*
  tunnels, *6, 7, 78,* 82, 85
  yard-long, 175
Beds, 23, 24
  deep, 31
  designing, *8,* 34–35, 123
  edging, 10, *41, 42,* 43–44, 47–49, 66, 105, *128,* 136, 176
  locations, 33
  orientation, 32–33, *143*
  perennial vegetables, 33
  raised, 2–3, 24–25, *24, 25,* 31
  reserve, 128, 133
  seed, 33–34, *139*
  shapes, *31,* 32, *32*
  sizes, 26, 31–32
  tall vegetables, 33
  traditional, 167

Beetroot, 9, 186
    'Bolthardy,' 171
Belgium, gardens in, *141*
Bell cloches, *9*, 116
Bergamot, 164
Berries
    black-, 53, 72, 85
    blue-, 30, 161, 163
    fruit cages, 86
    logan-, 53, 161, 169
    rasp-, 53, 160, 178
    See also Gooseberries;
        Strawberries
Binding gravel, 39
Birds, protecting berries from,
    86
Blackberries, 53, 72, 85
Black currants, 161
Block planting, 133
Blue, 161–63
Blueberries, 30, 161
    'Jersey,' 163
Borage, 163
Borders, 32
Bourgeois, Jacques, 111
Box, as bed edging, 10, *41*, *42*,
    49, 66, *128*
Brassicas, *44*, 46, 145
Brick, as bed edging, 49
Brick paths, *5*, 6–7, 39, *39*, *40*,
    102–4, *103*, 126, *126*
Brick walls, *54*, 55, *56*, *57*, 59
Broad beans, 157
Broccoli, 33, *44*, 46
    'Improved White
        Sprouting,' 157
    'Purple Sprouting,' 168
    'Regilio,' 157
    'Romanesco,' 159
    'Rosalind,' 168
Brogdale Experimental
    Horticultural Station, 82

Brown, Dennis, *81*, 82
Brussels sprouts, 46
    'Achilles,' 163
    'Bedford Asmer Monitor,'
        163
    blue, 163
    purple, 9
    red, 168
    'Rubine,' 168
Brynner, Mrs. Yul, garden of,
    109–11
Buchanan, Mr. and Mrs.
    Alistair, garden of, 73–76
Butterhead lettuce, *175*, 179
Buxus sempervirens. See Box

C

Cabbages, *44*, 46
    blue, 163
    'Celtix,' 163
    Chinese, 17, 157, 168, 176
    'Christmas,' 9
    colors, 46
    'Drumhead,' *2*, 9, 174
    'Gray Laird,' 148–49
    'Greyhound,' 9, 157
    harvesting, 142
    'Langedijker Early Norma,'
        168
    'Mizumi,' 164
    ornamental, 164, 178
    red, *161*, 168
    'Red Drumhead,' 156, 168
    Savoy, 163
    'Savoy King,' 178
    'Scarlett O'Hara,' 9
Cabot, Mr. and Mrs. Frank,
    garden of, *18*, 43–46, *43*,
    44, *45*, *48*, 118, 135–36,
    149

California, Walnut Creek,
    151–54, *151*, *152–53*, *154*,
    175
Canada, Les Quatre Vents, *18*,
    43–46, *43*, *44*, *45*, *48*, 118,
    135–36, *149*
Cardoons, 67
    'Violetta di Chioggia,' 157
Carrots, 82, *83*, 134, 136, 186
Carvalho, Ann, 2, 34
Carvalho, Joachim, 2, 34
Carvalho, Robert, 147
Catch cropping, 141–42
Catmint, 55, 58
Cauliflower
    'Elby,' 157
    'Purple Cape,' 168
    'Snowball,' 157
    'Violet Queen,' 168
Celery, 17
Chambers, Ann Cox, garden
    of, *31*, *48*, 61–63, *61*, *62*,
    63, *64*, *155*, *170*
Chapelle, garden of, *20*
Chard
    ruby, 9, 171
    Swiss, 9, 157, 178, 186
Charles, Prince of Wales, 82
    See also Highgrove
Chateau de Beauregard, *24*
Chateau de Miromesnil, *54*, *92*
Chateau de St. Jean-de-
    Beauregard, *91*
Chateau de Villandry. *See*
    Villandry, Chateau de
Chatsworth, 95
Cheesecloth cloches, *108*, 118
Cherries, 86
    'Marchiana,' 172
    'Merton Glory,' 169
    Morello, 18, 53
    sweet, 53

Chicory, 12, 67, 136
   'Alouette,' 168
   'Verona,' 9
China
   intercropping, 139
   raised beds, 24
Chinese cabbage, 17, 157, 168, 176
Chinese gooseberries, 86
Chives, 49, 164, 177, 186
   as bed edging, 10, 136
Cisterns, 101, 166–67, *167*
Citrus fruit, tunnels, 77–78
City gardens, 25, 185–86
Climbing flowers, 72, 82
Climbing fruits, 72
Climbing vegetables
   arbors, 71–72
   fences, 115
   locations, 33
   obelisks, 108, 113, 114
   tents, *107*, 108, 113, 140–41
   tepees, 108, 113, 114, 140–41
   tunnels, *6, 7*, 72, *77*, 85
   undercrops, 140–41
Cloches, 115–18
   cheesecloth, *108*, 118
   glass, *9, 97, 113*, 115–16
   plastic, 116–17
   polyethylene, 118
Close-planting, 134
Cobaea scandens 'Cathedral Bells,' 72
Cobnuts. *See* Hazelnut
Color, 147–49
   blocks of, 156
   contrasts, 149
   effects of light, 176
   of fruits, 147–48
   harmony, 148–49
   hot, 106, 171–72

   pale, 155
   perspective and, 149, 155
   schemes, 148, 152, 156
   strong, 155–56
   of vegetables, 147–49, 155–56
   See also specific colors
Compost heaps, 16
Concrete paths, 38–39, *38*
Concrete paving, 47
Concrete walls, 65
Connecticut
   Falls Village, *48*, 102–6, *102, 103, 104, 105, 108*
   Lakeville, *17, 40, 54*, 55–58, *55, 56, 57, 100*
Conservatory cases, 95
Containers, 107–8, 185–86
Cooking from the Garden (Creasey), 154
La Coquetterie, *25*, 123, 129–32, *129, 130–31, 132*
Cordons, 53, 175
Coriander, 136
Corn
   leaves, 177
   sweet, 18, 33, 67, 140
Corn salad, 136
Cornwall, Trengwainton, 25
Corylus maxima 'Purpurea,' 77
Cottager's kale, 164
The Country Housewife's Garden (Lawson), 4
Crab apple
   'Dartmouth,' 169
   'Golden Hornet,' 160
   'Veitch's Scarlet,' 172
Creasey, Rosalind, 154
Cress, 134
Cribier, Pascal, 132
Cromwell's Fort, 86
Cropping
   catch, 141–42

   inter-, 9, *133, 134*, 138–39
   mixed, 142
   planned, 134, 135–36, 138–42
   relay system, 139
   serial, 142
   under-, *137*, 140–41, *140*
Crop rotation, 26, 142–45
Cucumbers, 85
Curled kale, 178
Curly endive, 178
Currants, *129*
   black, 161
   hedges, 66
   red, 53, *170*, 172, 176
   white, 53, 158, 176
Cyclanthera pedata 'Edulis,' 46

D

Damson, 'Farleigh Damson,' 163
de Belders, garden, *141*
Deep beds, 31
Design, garden
   Barnsley, 9–12
   block planting, 133
   close-planting, 134
   focal points, 35
   form, 174–76
   with fruits and vegetables, 122–23, 128
   site selection, 15–19
   sources of ideas, 34–35
   texture, 176–79
   themes, 128
   vertical elements, 69–70
   See also Beds; Color
Dill, 136, 160, 178
Diseases, 144
Drainage, 17

Dwarf fruits
    apples, 53
    pears, 9, 53
    strawberries, *124*
    'Victoria' plums, 9
Dwarf hyssop, 49
Dwarf vegetables, 10, 152–54,
    185, 186

E

Eggplant, 179
Endive
    'Croquette,' 159
    curly, 178
England
    Barnsley House, 4–12
    Brogdale Experimental
        Horticultural Station,
        82
    Chatsworth, 95
    Highgrove, *70*, 79–82, *79,
        80, 81, 82*, 136, *162*
    Hillbarn House, 73–76, *73,
        74–75*, 118
    Hope End Hotel, *140*
    National Trust gardens, 25,
        86, 95, 114
    Peckover, 95
    Quarry Bank Hill, 128
    Stavordale Priory, *53*, 101,
        138, 156, 165–67, *165,
        166, 167*
    St. Mary's Farm, *37, 39, 71,
        123*
    Sudborough Old Rectory,
        26–30, *26, 27, 28, 29,
        38*, 136, 138, 145
    Thornbury Castle, 70
    Trengwainton, 25
    West Green House, 86

The English Flower Garden
    (Robinson), 52
Espaliers, 53
    pears, *81*
Evelyn, John, 142

F

Falls Village (Connecticut), *48,*
    102–6, *102, 103, 104, 105,
    108*
Fans, 53
Farrand, Beatrix, 6
Fences, 51–52
    bamboo, 64
    climbing vegetables on, 115
    iron, 65
    "junk," 64
    lattice, 64, 115
    materials, 52
    movable, 64
    ornamental, 114–15
    picket, 60, *60*
    timber, *59*, 60, *60*, 61–62, 64
Fennel, 17, 136, 160, 186
    Florence, 178
    purple, 171
Fenugreek, 134
Feverfew, 44
Field system, 23–24, *24*
Figs, 77, 108, 177
Filbert. *See* Hazelnut
Florence fennel, 178
Flowers
    climbing, 72, 82
    in containers, 108
    edible, 183
    of edible plants, 30
    table arrangements, 154
Forcing fruits and vegetables,
    115–18

Forcing jars, 118
Forms, 174–76
    architectural, 175
    fastigiate, 175
    globose, 176
    horizontal, 176
    indistinct, 174–75
    solid, 174
    weeping, 175
France
    Chateau de Beauregard, *24*
    Chateau de Miromesnil, *54,
        92*
    Chateau de St. Jean-de-
        Beauregard, *91*
    La Coquetterie, *25*, 123,
        129–32, *129, 130–31,
        132*
    Le Manoir de Criqueboef,
        109–11, *109, 110–11,
        133*
    La Petite Fontanille, *31, 48,*
        61–63, *61, 62, 63, 64,
        155, 170*
    Provence, 63
    Sceaux, 96
    Val Rahmeh, 86
    See also Villandry, Chateau
        de
Frederick, William, garden of,
    16
French beans, 82, 85, *158*, 159,
    168, 171
Frost
    pockets, 19, 52
    protection from, 19
Fruit cages, 86, 167
Fruits
    blue, 161, 163
    bushes, 33
    citrus, 77–78
    climbing, 72

colors, 147–48
dwarf, 9, 53, *124*
forcing, 115–18
forms, 175, 176
growing in greenhouses,
    92
hot colors, 172
leaf textures, 177, 178, 179
old varieties, 183
purple and red, 169
shade-tolerant, 16
South American, 106
supports, 115
tunnels, 85
white, silver, and gray, 158
yellow, 160
Fruit trees
    locations, 16, 33
    training, 7–9, 18, 53
    tunnels, 77–78, 79–82

G

Gainey, Ryan, 63
    garden of, *31, 101, 143*
Garden houses, 89–91, *90*, 96
Garden seats, 7, *100*, 101, 126,
    127
Garden structures
    greenhouses, 89–95, *91, 92*
    locations, 35
    potting sheds, 89–91,
        95–96
    toolsheds, *90, 93*
    See also Garden houses
Garlic, 177
Givenchy, Hubert, 96
Glass cloches, *9, 97, 113,*
    115–16
Glazed cases, 95
Glazed frames, 95

Glin Castle, *47, 90*, 118, *118*
Globe artichokes, 32, 33, 186
Golden marjoram, 160
Golden purslane, 134
Golden thyme, 49, 160
Gooseberries, *7, 9*, 176
    'Careless,' 158
    Chinese, 86
    hedges, 66
    'Laxton's Amber,' 160
    'May Duke,' 169
    training on walls, 18, 53
    'Whinhan's Industry,' 169
    'Whitesmith,' 158
Gourds
    in borders, 32
    tunnels, *6, 7, 77*
    See also Squashes
Graded gravel, 40
Grapevines, 72, 86
Grass, as bed edging, 49
Grass paths, 38, *38*
Gravel paths, 39–42, 47
Gray, 156–58
Great burdock, 177
Greengages, 53, 86
    'Count Althana's,' 169
    dwarf pyramids, 175
    'Oullins,' 160
Greenhouses, 89–95, *91, 92*
Greve, Ineke, garden of, *65,*
    124–27, *124, 125, 126,*
    127

H

Hanging baskets, 108
Harvesting. *See* Cropping
Hazelnut, tunnels, 72, *74–75,*
    76, 77
Hazel rods, 70, *70*, 71

Hedges, 51–52, 65–66, *65*
    box, *41, 42*
    evergreen, 66, *66*
    as windscreens, 66
    yew, *66*
Henry Doubleday Research
    Association, 183
Herb gardens
    at Stavordale Priory, 166
    at Te Doom, 124–25, *126*
Herbs
    as bed edging, 49, 66, 136
    blue, 163
    in containers, 108
    leaf textures, 178
    pink and mauve, 164
    purple and red, 171
    undercrops, 140
    white, silver, and gray, 157,
        158
    yellow, 160
Hewat, Christopher, 57
High barn cloches, 116
Highgrove, *70*, 79–82, *79, 80,*
    81, 82, 136, *162*
Hillbarn House, 73–76
    nut tunnel, 72, *74–75*, 76
    pear arches, 72, 74
    quince arches, 73–74, *73*
    topiary, 118
History, garden design ideas
    from, 34
Hoggin, 39–40
Holland, Te Doom, *65,*
    124–27, *124, 125, 126,*
    127
Hope End Hotel, *140*
Horseradish, 32, 33
Hot colors, 106, 171–72
Huntington, Mr. and Mrs.,
    garden of, 26

I

Intercropping, 9, *133*, *134*, 138–39
Ireland
    Cromwell's Fort, 86
    Glin Castle, *47*, *90*, 118, *118*
    Leixlip Castle, *100*
    Shackleton, *113*
Iron arbors, 70, 71–72
Iron fences, 65
Islamic art, 35, *35*, *36*
Italy
    Abbadia a Coltibuono, 78
    Villa Carlotta, 78

J

Japanese spring
    chrysanthemum, 134
Jefferson, Thomas, 96
Jekyll, Gertrude, 32, 161, 186
Jerusalem Artichokes, 33, 67
Johnson, Hugh, 181–82

K

Kale, *44*, 46
    cottager's, 164
    curled, 178
    'Rugged Jack,' 168
    sea, 32, 163, 177
    'Westland Autumn,' 163
Keen, Lady Mary, garden of, *37*, *123*
Kitchen gardens
    accessibility, 18, 33
    benefits, 181–83
    popularity, 2–3
    sizes, 20, 185

    techniques, 183–85
    time needed, 185
    winter appearance, 10–12
    See also Design; Sites
Kiwi, 86, 177
Kohlrabi, 46
    'Purple Vienna,' 168
    'Rolano,' 163

L

Lablab beans, *6*, 7
Lake Como, 78
Lakeville (Connecticut), *17*, *40*, *54*, 55–58, *55*, *56*, *57*, *100*
Lamb's lettuce, 128
Langton, Mr. and Mrs., garden of, 165–67, *165*, *167*
Lantern cloches, 115
Larkcom, Joy, 183
Last, John, 73, 74
Lattice fences, 64, 115
Lavender, 157, *165*
    as bed edging, 9, 49, 66, 105, *105*
    dwarf, 9, 105
Lawson, William, 4, *10*
Leaves
    feathery, 178
    grassy, 177
    large, 177
    rough-textured, 178
    smooth-textured, 179
    soft-textured, 179
    sword, 177
Le Brun, Charles, 96
Leeks, 177
    'Blue Solaise,' 168
    'Cortina,' 163
    'Musselborough,' 9

Leixlip Castle, *100*
Lemon balm, 160
Lemon grass, 177
Leningrad, 186
Lettuce
    'Apache,' 168
    bolted, *81*, *82*, 136
    butterhead, *175*, 179
    colors, 151–52, *152–53*, *154*
    dwarf, 10, 186
    'Feuilles de Chene,' 169
    forms, 175
    harvesting, 136
    intercropping with strawberries, 9
    lamb's, 128
    'Lollo Bionda,' 159
    'Lollo Rosso,' 169
    'May Queen,' 168
    'Panella Red,' 169
    'Rougette du Midi,' 169
    'Trotzkoph,' 168
Loganberries, 53, 161
    'LT59,' 169
Long Island (New York), *64*
Low barn cloches, 116
Lufkin, Elise, garden of, *17*, *40*, *54*, 55–58, *55*, *56*, *57*, *100*
Lupins, 12, 167, *167*

M

Le Manoir de Criqueboef, 109–11, *109*, *110–11*, *133*
Marigolds, 149
    dwarf, 44
Mauve, 164
McCabe, Nancy, 55
    garden of, *48*, 101, 102–6, *102*, *103*, *104*, *105*, *108*, *176*

Meager, Leonard, 34
Medieval gardens, 63, 144
Merton, Mrs. Ralph, garden
    of, *38*
Miromesnil, Chateau de, *54,*
    92
Mixed cropping, 142
Modern art, 35
Mondrian, Piet, 35, *36*
Monticello (Virginia), garden
    house, 96
Morello cherry, 18, 53
Moscow, 186
Mount Vernon (Virginia), 101
    garden house, 96
    picket fences, *60*
Mudd's Restaurant, 151–54,
    151, 152–53, 154, 175
Mulch, 24, 47, 156
Mustard, 134

N

Nasturtiums, 7, 72, *149,* 176
National Trust gardens, 114
    Peckover, 95
    Trengwainton, 25
    West Green House, 86
Nectarines, 53
Nepeta 'Six Hills Giant,' *55,*
    58
The Netherlands, Te Doom,
    65, 124–27, *124, 125,*
    126, 127
New Orchard and Garden
    (Lawson), *10*
The New Arte of Gardening
    (Meager), 34
New York, Long Island, *64*
Nut tunnels, 72, *74–75,* 76, 77

O

Obelisks, 108, 113, 114
Ogden, Shep, garden of, *161*
Okra, 'Long Green,' 159
Onions, 134, 177
    in crop rotation plans, 145
    'Ishekuro,' 163
    'Winter White Bunching,'
        163
Oriental poppies, 167
Ornaments, garden, 99–101
    antiques, 101, 102, 104,
        166–67
    witty, 118

P

Page, Russell, 128, 130
Parsley, 10, 49, 186
Passiflora edulis, 86
Passion fruit, 86
Paths, 35–36
    brick, *5,* 6–7, 39, *39, 40,*
        102–4, *103,* 126, *126*
    concrete, 38–39, *38,* 47
    grass, 38, *38*
    gravel, 39–42, 47
    material colors, 30
    materials, 38–42
    stone, 47, *47*
    widths, 36
Pavilion of Aurora, Sceaux, 96
Peaches
    'Peregrine,' 179
    training on walls, 18, 53, *56*
    weeping, 175
Pea gravel, 40
Pears
    arches, 72, 74
    cordons, 53, 175

dwarf, 9, 53
espaliers, *81*
leaves, 179
'Packham's Triumph,' 160
training on walls, 18, 53,
    82
tunnels, 72, 77
Peas, 186
    'Purple-Podded,' 169
Peckover, 95
Pelargonium, 179
Peppers
    'Luteus,' 159
    red, 172
    sweet, 172
    yellow, 159, 172
Perennial vegetables, 33
Pergolas, 69, *84,* 85–86
Perilla, 179
    'Red,' 169
Pests, 144
La Petite Fontanille, 61–63,
    61, 62, 63, 64, 155, 170
    bed edgings, *48*
    bed shapes, *31*
Picket fences, 60, *60*
Pink, 164
Planned cropping, 134,
    135–36, 138–42
Plant rotation. *See* Crop rotation
Plastic cloches, 116–17
Plums, 86
    dwarf, 9
    dwarf pyramids, 175
    'Kirbe's Blue,' 163
    'Pershore Egg,' 160
    training on walls, 53, *162*
    'Victoria,' 9, 27, 169
    yellow, 160
Les Plus Excellents Bastiments de
    France, 34

Polyethylene cloches, 118
Potatoes, in crop rotation
    plans, 145
Potting sheds, 89–91, 95–96
Prevosteau, Jacques, 111
Provence, 63
    La Petite Fontanille, *31, 48,
        61–63, 61, 62, 63, 64,
        155, 170*
Prunus persica 'Windle
    Weeping,' 175
Pulses, 145
Pumpkins, 171
Purple, 168–71

Q

Quadripods, 114
Les Quatre Vents, *18,* 43–46,
    43, 44, 45, 48, 118,
    135–36, *149*
Quebec. *See* Quatre Vents
Quince
    arches, 73–74, *73*
    rods, 71

R

Rabbits, protection from,
    131–32
Radicchio, 179
Raised beds, 2–3, 24–25, *24,
    25,* 31
Raspberries, 53, 178
    'Golden Everest,' 160
    yellow, 160
Red, 168–71
Red currants, 53, *170,* 172,
    176
Red orach, 169

Reserve beds, 128, 133
Retaining walls, 43–44
Rhubarb, 32, 33, 177
    'Hawke's Champagne,' 169
Robinson, William, 52, 116
Root crops, in crop rotation
    plans, 145
Roper, Lanning, 73
Rosemary, 49, 66, 157, 158,
    163
Roses, 'Iceberg,' 9, 156
Rotation. *See* Crop rotation
Rothschild, Lady, garden of,
    19, 66, 114, 116–17, 150
Rubus laciniatus 'Oregon
    Thornless,' 72, 85
Ruby chard, 9, 171
Runner beans, 7, 32, 72, 85,
    114, 157, 164, 169, 171,
    186

S

Sage, 49, 157, 158
    as bed edging, 66, 136
    purple, 49, 171
Salad crops
    in crop rotation plans, 145
    seed mixtures, 142
Saladino, John, garden of, *90*
Salad onions, 163
Salad rape, 134
Salisbury, Lady, 82
Salix alba 'Hakura Mishuka,'
    26, 27
Salsify, 'Mammoth,' 169
Savoy cabbage, 163, 178
Scarecrows, 44, *44,* 118, *118*
Sceaux (France), 96
Scorzonera, 186
Sculpture, 99–100

Sea kale, 32, 163, 177
Seed beds, 33–34, *139*
Seed guardians, 183
Seedling crops, 134
Seeds, mixtures, 142
Self-sown seedlings, 12, 128
Serial cropping, 142
Shackleton, *113*
Shade, fruits tolerant of, 16
Shingle, 40–42
Silver, 156–58
Sites
    selecting, 15–19
    sloping, 16, 33, 43–44
Soil, 17
Sorrel, 33
South American vegetables
    and fruits, 106
Southernwood, 49
Spinach, wild, 33
Squashes, 46, 176
    in borders, 32
    leaves, 177
    'Red Kuri,' 172
    summer, 159
    tunnels, 85
    'Turk's Turban,' 172
    See also Gourds
Stavordale Priory, *53,* 101,
    138, 156, 165–67, *165,
    166, 167*
St. Jean-de-Beauregard,
    Chateau de, *91*
St. Mary's Farm, *37, 39, 71,
    123*
Stokes' catalog, 46
Stone, as bed edging, 47, *47*
Stone paths, 47, *47*
Stone walls, 53, *53*
Strawberries, 124
    alpine, 10, 49, 160, 176
    'Cambridge Favorite,' 172

dwarf, *124*
intercropping with lettuce, 9
mulching, 111
Strawberry barrels, 108, *124*
Sudborough Old Rectory,
    26–30, *26, 27, 28*
    beds, 136
    cropping, 138
    paths, *38*
    plan, *29*, 145
Summer squashes, 159
Sunflowers, 7, 67
Sunlight, 16, 33
Sweet cicely, 178
Sweet corn, 18, 33, 67, 140
Sweet peas, 72, 82
Sweet peppers, 172
Swiss chard, 9, 157, 178, 186
Systema Horti-culturae
    (Worlidge), 34, *34*

T

Te Doom, *65*, 124–27, *124,
    125, 126, 127*
Tent cloches, *113*, 116
Tents, *107*, 108, 113, 140–41
Tepees, 108, 113, 114, 140–41
Texture, 176–79
Thornbury Castle, 70
Thyme, 49, 158, 186
Tile, as bed edging, *48*, 49,
    104
Timber, as bed edging, *43, 44,
    48*, 49
Timber fences, *59*, 60, *60*,
    61–62, 64
Timber walls, 43–44, 60
Tomatoes, 186
    in Canada, 46
    'Gardener's Delight,' 172

'Golden Boy,' 159
'Golden Sunrise,' 159
'Tiny Tim,' 172
yellow, 159
Toolsheds, *90, 93*
Topiary, *77*, 118
Trelliswork, 111
    arbors, 70, 71
Trengwainton, 25
Tripods, 114
Tropaeolum canariense, 72
Tudor, Tasha, garden of, *78*
Tunnels, 69–70, *70*, 72, 79–82
    at Barnsley, *6, 7, 72, 77*
    beans, *6, 7, 78*, 82, 85
    fruits, 77–78, *79–82*, 85
    nut, 72, *74–75*, 76, 77
    pear, 72
    vegetables, *6*, 7, 72, *77*, 85
    vines, 78

U

Umbellifers, in crop rotation
    plans, 145
Under-cropping, *137*, 140–41,
    140
United States
    Atlanta (Georgia), *31, 101,
        143*
    Falls Village (Connecticut),
        48, 102–6, *102, 103,
        104, 105, 108*
    Lakeville (Connecticut), *17,
        40, 54*, 55–58, *55, 56,
        57, 100*
    Long Island (New York),
        64
    Monticello (Virginia), 96
    Mount Vernon (Virginia),
        60, 96, 101

Walnut Creek (California),
    151–54, *151, 152–53,
    154, 175*
University of California-Davis,
    25
Utens, Edward, 34, *35*

V

Val Rahmeh, 86
Variegated lemon balm, 160
Vegetables
    annual, 33
    blue, 161, 163
    colors, 147–49, 155–56
    in containers, 108, 185–86
    dwarf, 10, 152–54, 185, 186
    field system, 23–24, *24*
    forcing, 115–18
    forms, 175, 176
    hardy, 46
    hot colors, 106, 171–72
    leaf textures, 177–79
    new varieties, 185
    old varieties, 183
    perennial, 33
    pink and mauve, 164
    purple and red, 168–69
    raising from seed, 33–34
    South American, 106
    supports, 115
    tall, 33, 115
    undercrops, 140–41
    white, silver, gray, 157
    whole, 152–54
    winter, 10–12
    yellow, 159
    See also Climbing vegetables
Verey, Rosemary, 4–12, 30, 34,
    63, 142
    See also Barnsley House

Villa Carlotta, 78
Villandry, Chateau de, 2, *2*, 9,
        21
    beds, *24*
    box hedges, *41, 42*
    cropping, 138
    garden design, 34, *122*, 123
Vines
    on arbors, 7, 72
    grape, 72, 86
    on pergolas, 86
    on tepees, 114
    tunnels, 78
Virginia
    Monticello, 96
    Mount Vernon, *60*, 96, 101
Vitis 'Brant,' 72
Vitis vinifera
    'Apifolia,' 72
    'Dusty Miller,' 179
    'Purpurea,' 72

W

Wall germander, 49
Walls, 51–52
    brick, *54*, 55, *56, 57*, 59
    concrete, 65

fruit tree support, 18, 53
    materials, 52
    retaining, 43–44
    stone, 53, *53*
    timber, 43–44, 60
Walnut Creek (California),
        151–54, *151, 152–53, 154,
        175*
Washington, George, 96
Wasps, 12
Water, 17
    drainage, 17
    ornamental pools, 17
    rain, 18
Welsh onion, 157
West Green House, 86
White, 156–58
White currants, 53, 158, 176
Williams, Mrs. Bunny
    garden of, *17, 48, 59, 84,
        100, 101*
    toolshed, *93*
Willow rods, 70, 71
Wind
    and bed orientation, 33
    breaks, 19, 67
    protection from, 18, 52, 66
Winter savory, 49
Winter vegetables, 10–12

Wit, in garden ornaments, 118
Wood. *See* Timber
Worlidge, John, 34, *34*, 70–71

Y

Yang, Linda, 185
Yard-long beans, 175
Yellow, 158–60

Z

Zucchini, 182
    'Gold Rush,' 159